Big Book Study Guide

Russell Forrest, MA

Grateful acknowledgment is made for permission to reprint the following:

"Dr. Silkworth's Rx for Sobriety." Published in the *AA Grapevine,* June 1945. Copyright © June 1945 by the AA Grapevine, Inc. Reprinted with permission of AA Grapevine, Inc.

Excerpt from *Lois Remembers.* Copyright © 1979 by Al-Anon Family Group Headquarters, Inc. Reprinted with permission of Al-Anon Family Group Headquarters, Inc.

Excerpts from *Bill W.* Copyright © 1975 by Robert Thomsen. Reprinted by permission of Hazelden Foundation.

Excerpts from *What Is The Oxford Group.* Copyright © 1997 by Hazelden Foundation. Reprinted by permission of Hazelden Foundation.

Excerpt from *A Program For You* by Joe Mc. and Charlie P. Copyright © 1991 by Hazelden Foundation. Reprinted by permission of Hazelden Foundation.

Excerpts from *The Addictive Personality* by Craig Nakken. Copyright © 1988, 1996 by Hazelden Foundation. Reprinted by permission of Hazelden Foundation.

Excerpt from *New Wine* by Mel B. Copyright © 1991 by Hazelden Foundation. Reprinted by permission of Hazelden Foundation.

Excerpts from *Silkworth - The Little Doctor Who Loved Drunks,* by Dale Mitchel. Copyright © 2002 by Hazelden Foundation. Reprinted by permission of Hazelden Foundation.

Excerpt from *Bill W.: A Biography of Alcoholics Anonymous Cofounder Bill Wilson* by Francis Hartigan. Copyright © 2001 by Francis Hartigan. Reprinted by permission of St. Martin's Press.

Excerpts from *Victims & Sinners – Spiritual Roots of Addiction and Recovery* by Linda A. Mercadante. Copyright © 1996 by Linda A. Mercadante. Reprinted by permission of Westminster John Knox Press.

For the Jellinek patients –

I stayed up all night reading that book. For me it was a wonderful experience. It explained so much I had not understood about myself and, best of all, it promised recovery if I would do a few simple things and be willing to have the desire to drink removed. Here was hope. Maybe I could find my way out of this agonizing existence. Perhaps I could find freedom and peace and be able once again to call my soul my own.

Sylvia K., "The Keys of the Kingdom"

The genius of AA is that it attends to the alcoholic – *not* her alcoholism. It understands the need to compensate her for laying down the bottle, the need to reward her abstinence with sobriety, and the need to substitute spiritual sustenance for denied spirits.

Big Book Study Guide, 153

Connection is the antidote to intoxication.

Big Book Study Guide, Appendices A, C

Contents

Introduction

The Big Book is not an easy book. It is a mix of science and philosophy, spirituality and psychology, self-survey and personal revelation. It advocates for alcoholism as an illness, yet points the reader to a Power greater than herself for solution to this illness. It shows the alcoholic how to arrest his alcohol problem, only to introduce him to himself as the original and ongoing problem. Its language, while occasionally colorful and even poetic, is often foreign to the modern ear. Its suggested remedy, while lifesaving, is not easy to swallow or sustain. One cannot understand the book without understanding some important truths about one's self and one's drinking. These truths alone, however, will not save one from the bottle. Yet between the Big Book's cover lies the same suggested road out of King Alcohol's mad realm that has been taken by battered souls since 1939. It is not an easy road, but recovery demands of one a choosing. Ultimately, many an alcoholic has come to be grateful for this push.

A study guide to the Big Book seems destined to run afoul of fact and interpretation. What the authors *intended* to communicate in any given paragraph may be subject to question; what these same paragraphs *actually* say may be equally open to debate. In either case, what errors of fact I am guilty of I hope are few and of small consequence. Mistakes of interpretation, on the other hand, I hope prove exciting and provoking, not boring or lazy.

I wish to thank the chemical dependency clinicians, mental health and clergy persons, recreational specialists, counselors-in-training, nurses, and housekeepers that it was my great fortune to work with during my tenure in Hazelden's extended recovery program – *Jellinek* – in Center City, Minnesota. Thanks to Damian McElrath for his unflinching support of the Jellinek staff and clients, and his assistance in editing the study guide's manuscript. Thanks also to Linda Mercadante for her book, *Victims and Sinners.* Her words on grace and sin helped deepen my understanding of the problem of *self,* and AA's spiritual remedy for the alcoholic's misadventure with the bottle.

Last, a very special thank you to all the patients in Jellinek Hall who allowed me to be part of their stories during the eighteen plus years I served on their behalf. It is to these spirited and spiritual travelers, past and present, that I dedicate this guide.

Whether a newcomer to AA or a seasoned traveler on the Road of Happy Destiny, whether you have a pristine, dog-eared, or dust-covered Big Book, it is my hope that this study guide helps illuminate the text where illumination seems needed, excites considered discussion, and awakens some delicious spiritual truths.

Introduction to Second Edition

It's been fourteen or so years since the first edition of this guide saw the sun. Originally to be published by Hazelden-Pittman Archives Press, it fell victim to copyright problems and, never finding another publisher, was neatly boxed (along with supporting documents) and stored.

To be sure, I'd occasionally bump into it (chiefly when moving); take it out to review and reminisce, to trim a little fat here or do a little something there; and then, after a respectful number of days, return it to a new, clean box.

A recent job rekindled my interest in the guide and twelve-step philosophy; specifically, the critical role of connection in recovery and spiritual renewal, and its relationship with secure attachment. This, combined with the walk of time ("Hey, do something with it, already") helped kick start my work on this second edition.

I've tweaked the section on Big Book Recovery Philosophy, and added appendices on alcoholism as an intimacy disorder, spiritual awakenings, and myths and misconceptions about AA. And as with the initial offering, I again shied away from advise and opinion about the so-called treatment industry.

Last, sometime during the night or day it hit me: I started out to write a guide through *Alcoholics Anonymous;* I finished up with guide and commentary. Hopefully the combination proves a win-win for the reader.

Style and Content

A word or two on the use of this guide: First, this guide is just that: *a guide*. It is neither exhaustive, definitive nor a suitable substitute for actually immersing oneself in the "basic text." Half measures avail one nothing. No responsibility will be assumed for any spiritual ill resulting from bypassing the Big Book itself.

Big Book citations have been taken from the first and second editions, which exist in the public domain. The same holds true for selections from Personal Stories (some of which have also been carried over into the third and fourth editions). Pagination for the recovery portion of the second, third, and fourth editions (Chapters 1 to 11, or pages 1 to 164) are identical, allowing for ease in cross-referencing. The numbering (Roman numerals) of the Preface, the Forewords to First and Second Editions, and the "The Doctor's Opinion" is, however, somewhat different in editions two, three and four.

I have elected to alternate gender pronouns instead of adhering to the text's heavy use of the masculine pronoun or adopting a gender-neutral format. I believe it important that female alcoholics receive equal billing with their male counterparts, and that both not be collectively homogenized into the third-person plural. I have also chosen to include footnotes and citations in the body of the text, rather than have the reader hunt them down in the back pages. I hope that both choices prove user-friendly.

The study guide's format follows that of the Big Book, second edition: Preface, Forewords to First and Second Editions, "The Doctor's Opinion," and Chapters 1 to 11. Abbreviations include "Mid." for the middle of the page, and "Bot." for the bottom. One character used through the guide – ☞ – indicates additional commentary on a concept, line, paragraph, etc. Unless otherwise indicated, numbers given in parentheses refer to Big Book pages.

A final remark: At some point in the writing of this guide I needed to make a decision to put down the pen and go to press. As such, this guide remains a work in progress. Folks seeking a more comprehensive account of Alcoholics Anonymous (program or text) might begin with several titles published by Alcoholics Anonymous World Services, Inc., chiefly *Pass It On – The Story of Bill Wilson and How the A.A. Message Reached the World, Dr. Bob and the Good Oldtimers,* and *A.A. Comes of Age.* Dick B. has done an admirable job detailing the influence of the Oxford Group, scripture, and the Rev. Sam Shoemaker on the birth of AA and its Twelve Step philosophy in *Turning Point – A History of Early A.A.'s Spiritual Roots and Successes,* and *The Oxford Group and Alcoholics Anonymous.* Several interesting titles, especially biographies of persons linked to AA's formative years, have also been published by Hazelden Pittman Archives Press.

Abbreviations

AAC - "A.A. At The Crossroads"

AACA - *Alcoholics Anonymous Comes of Age*

AP - *The Addictive Personality* (Second Edition)

AAS - *AA: The Story*

AAWB - *AA: The Way It Began*

BBD - *Big Book Discussion*

BFQ - *Bartlett's Familiar Quotations* (Sixteenth Edition)

BW - *Bill W.*

BWB - *Bill W.: A Biography of Alcoholics Anonymous Cofounder Bill Wilson*

CC - *Courage to Change*

CEO - *Compton's Encyclopedia Online v3.0*

DB - *Dr. Bob and the Good Oldtimers*

DSM - *Diagnostic Criteria from DSM-5*

EBBY - *Ebby: The Man Who Sponsored Bill*

EP - *The Encyclopedia of Philosophy*

FA - *The Family and Alcoholism*

GSB - *General Service Board of Alcoholics Anonymous, Inc.*

LG - *Loosening the Grip*

LH - *The Language of the Heart*

LR - *Lois Remembers*

NA - *Narcotics Anonymous*

NG - *Not-God*

NW - *New Wine*

OGAA - *The Oxford Group & Alcoholics Anonymous*

PD - *The Psychopathology of Denial*

PIO - *Pass It On*

PS - *The Promises of Sobriety*

PTP - *Practice These Principles* and *What Is The Oxford Group?*

RG - *A Reference Guide to the Big Book of Alcoholics Anonymous*

RLT - *The Road Less Traveled*

S - *Silkworth – The Little Doctor Who Loved Drunks*

SS - *Sexual Solutions*

TP - *Turning Point*

12X12 - *Twelve Steps and Twelve Traditions*

VRE - *The Varieties of Religious Experience*

VS - *Victims & Sinners*

WP - *Women Pioneers in Twelve Step Recovery*

Cast of Characters

Key figures in the early history of Alcoholics Anonymous include:

William Griffith Wilson ("Bill W.") - Co-founder, Alcoholics Anonymous. Born November 26, 1895, in East Dorset, Vermont (in a room behind the bar of the Wilson House, the village hotel run by his grandmother). (*PIO,* 13) Died January 24, 1971. Buried in East Dorset Cemetery. Stockbroker and investment analyst. Husband to Lois Burnham (1918 - 1971). No children. Three treatments for alcoholism at Towns Hospital in New York City (1933 to 1934). Last drink: December 11, 1934, at age 39.

Lois Burnham Wilson - Co-founder, Al-Anon (with Anne B.), 1951. Born March 4, 1891, at her family's home at 182 Clinton Street, Brooklyn, New York. Died October 5, 1988. Buried in East Dorset Cemetery. Her memoirs have been captured in *Lois Remembers.* These words come from the book's Preface:

> "Bill's recovery came about in spite of me. Although it was what I had been working for all our married life, I had gone about it the wrong way. My love, as deep as it was, was also possessive; and my ego was so great I felt I could change him into what I thought he ought to be." (©1979, Al-Anon Family Group Head-quarters, Inc. Reprinted with permission of Al-Anon Family Group Headquarters, Inc.)

Robert Holbrook Smith, MD ("Dr. Bob") - Co-founder, Alcoholics Anonymous. Born August 8, 1879, in St. Johnsbury, Vermont (seventy-five miles north of Bill's birthplace). Died November 16, 1950. Buried in Mt. Peace Cemetery, Akron, Ohio. Physician and surgeon. A graduate of Dartmouth College (1902) and Rush Medical School (1910). (*DB, 22, 27*) Later trained at Mayo Clinic in Rochester, Minnesota, and Jefferson Medical School in Philadelphia to specialize in proctology and rectal surgery. Husband to Anne Ripley Smith. Two children: Robert "Smitty," and Sue (adopted). Introduced to Bill W. on May 12, 1935 (Mother's Day) by Henrietta Seiberling. Last drink: traditionally given as June 10, 1935 (AA's birthday or "Founder's Day") at age 55.

Anne Ripley Smith - Born 1879; died June 1, 1949. Buried in Mt. Peace Cemetery. Described by Bill as the "mother" of AA's first group (*LH,* 353), in part for her work with alcoholics (the Smith's house at 855 Ardmore Avenue in Akron "became a hostel for would-be AA members") (*WP,* 1); in part for the influence of her ideas on the birthing of AA (*WP,* 2). Declined Bill's invitation to write Chapter 8, "To Wives," in the Big Book. (*AAWB,* 180) *Anne Smith's Spiritual Workbook,* comprising her own reflections on

Oxford Group principles and Christian literature, has been published by Glen Abby Books.

Carl Jung - (1875-1961) Swiss psychiatrist. Prescribes religious conversion experience to **Rowland Hazard** ("a certain American business man," (26)) as an antidote to Roland's alcohol obsession (1931). Rowland subsequently finds conversion through his involvement in the Oxford Group, and later schools Bill's friend, **Edwin Thacher,** in Oxford Group tenets (August 1934).

Edwin "Ebby" Thacher - Born April 29, 1896, in Albany, New York. (*Ebby,* 20) Died March 21, 1966. (*Ebby,* 135) A school friend and occasional drinking buddy of Bill W. Member of Oxford Group; later Alcoholics Anonymous. Carries message of hope and salvation to Bill in November 1934. Has intermittent periods of abstinence between August 1934 (initial exposure to Oxford Group) and his death in 1966 (approximately two and one-half years). (*Ebby,* 149)

William D. "Silky" Silkworth, MD - (1873-1951) Medical Superintendent, Towns Hospital, 293 Central Park West, New York City (1932 to 1945); later Director of Alcoholic Treatment, Knickerbocker Hospital, New York City (1945-51). Speaks of alcoholism as an allergy of the body *and* an obsession of the mind. Writes two letters that comprise "The Doctor's Opinion" in the Big Book. A tireless helper of alcoholics and one of the earliest medical voices to champion Alcoholics Anonymous. Affectionately referred to as "the little doctor who loved drunks." (*S,* xiii)

William James, MD - (1842-1910) American physician, philosopher, and psychologist. His *The Varieties of Religious Experience* was recommended reading for members of the Oxford Group. Bill W. is given a copy of the book (by Ebby or Rowland) while at Towns Hospital in December 1935. Its two chapters on conversion help provide context and credibility to Bill's own "hot flash" or "white light" experience. (*PIO,* 125) Reference to James may be found on page 28 and in Appendix II of the Big Book.

Sam Shoemaker - (1893-1963) American leader of the Oxford Group and Rector of Calvary Episcopal Church in New York City (1921-1952). Church operated Calvary Rescue Mission (Ebby's residence during the time he carried a message of recovery to Bill), and Calvary House (Oxford Group headquarters in the United States, and site of Oxford Group meetings attended by Bill and Lois in the mid-1930s). Regarded by Bill as one of the co-founders of AA for helping pass on many of the spiritual tenets woven into the twelve steps. (*A.A. Grapevine,* January 1964)

Frank Buchman - American Lutheran minister (1871 - 1961) and founder of the **Oxford Group** 1922), a nondenominational, evangelical movement which aimed to recapture the fervor, "the beliefs and methods of the Apostles." (*OGAA*, 63) Members sought spiritual rebirth through rigorous moral inventory, confession of shortcomings, restitution for harm done, helpfulness to others, and surrender to and dependence upon God. (xvi) Its Four Absolutes (Purity, Honesty, Unselfishness, Love), "the keys to the kind of spiritual life God wishes us to lead" (*PTP,* Book II, 6), still survive in Akron/Cleveland AA circles. (*NW, 95*) Though not dedicated to helping alcoholics, many did find relief from their destructive obsession through the Oxford Group's emphasis on "change" or religious conversion. Called "A First Century Christian Fellowship" up to 1928; thereafter the Oxford Group until it's final incarnation as Moral Re-Armament in 1938. (*NW, 37, 44*)

Birth of the Book

1. **What is the Big Book?** The Big Book is the "basic text" of Alcoholics Anonymous. Initially published in April 1939, it formalized and formally introduced AA's twelve-step prescription for alcoholism.

The Big Book might also be considered from these standpoints:

• An Exodus Story - It is the story of how an anonymous group of men and women found *a way out* of King Alcohol's mad realm. (See the title page: *Alcoholics Anonymous – The Story of How Many Thousands of Men and Women Have Recovered from Alcoholism*).

☞ Contrary to the cries of some of its greatest detractors, and words of some its biggest fans, neither Alcoholics Anonymous the book, nor Alcoholics Anonymous the organization, has ever claimed that their way is the only way. (Readers may, of course, encounter individuals at meetings who make such a claim, perhaps adding the additional claim that the way they do or understand the only way is the only way to do or understand it!). The following words from Foreword to Second Edition should help dispel this misconception:

"Upon therapy for the alcoholic himself, we surely have no monopoly. Yet it is our great hope that all those who have as yet found no answer may begin to find one on the pages of this book and will presently join us on the highroad to a new freedom."

• A Witness to God's Power - A demonstration that "God could and would [relieve us of our alcohol obsession] if He were sought." (60) This theme of witnessing for God finds expression in the "Third Step Prayer" on page 63: ". . . Take away my difficulties, that victory over them may bear witness to those I might help of Thy Power, Thy Love, and Thy Way of life. May I do Thy will always!"

• A Twelfth-step call on the still suffering alcoholic – Thus from page 19:

"If we [AA's founding fellowship] keep on the way we are going there is little doubt that much good will result, but the surface of the problem would hardly be scratched. Those of us who live in large cities are overcome by the reflection that close by hundreds are dropping into oblivion every day. Many could recover if they had the opportunity we have enjoyed. How then shall we present that which has been so freely given us? "We have concluded to publish an anonymous volume [*Alcoholics Anonymous*] setting forth the problem as we see it. We shall bring to the task our combined experience and knowledge. This should suggest a useful program for anyone concerned with a drinking problem."

When the reader studies the text and does as it prescribes, she is in effect admitting to the *problem,* aligning herself (her will) to its *solution,* and allowing herself to be twelve-stepped into recovery.

• A Political Statement - The text helped popularize the idea of alcoholism as rooted in illness, not badness, weakness or absence of moral fiber. It also helped legitimize the alcoholic's claim for public acceptance of her illness.

2. Is "Big Book" the real name of the book? No. The Big Book is actually the affectionate nickname given to the book, *Alcoholics Anonymous,* by early AAs. (Preface) Indeed, it was from the book's title that the young fellowship took its name. (*PIO,* 203) (Debate exists as to the identity of the first individual group to call itself Alcoholics Anonymous. Clarence S. claimed that the Cleveland group he found in May 1939 held this honor. (*PIO,* 203))

3. When was *Alcoholics Anonymous* published? The first edition, first printing of *Alcoholics Anonymous* was published in April 1939 by Works Publishing of New York City, a stock company formed in 1938 by Henry "Hank" Parkhurst to help finance its cost. (*PIO,* 194-195) (Hank's story, "The Unbeliever," appeared in the first edition.) It was printed by the Cornwall Press Company, Inc., in Cornwall, New York. Roughly 5,000 copies were printed (4,650 per www.abookman.com). The book contained 400 pages, including a recovery program for the alcoholic (the opening half of the text); a "Personal Stories" or testimonial section (the second half); and a two-page Appendix introducing The Alcoholic Foundation, and offering details on how to order the book and correspond with the Foundation. A brief Foreword setting down the "main purpose" of the book ("To show other alcoholics *precisely how we have recovered . . .*") was also included. In total, there were 30 personal histories, including "A Feminine Victory" (the story of Florence R., the first female member of AA), and "An Alcoholic's Wife" ("I have the misfortune, or should I say good fortune of being an alcoholic's wife. I say misfortune because of the worry and grief that goes with drinking, and good fortune because we found a new way of living." (378)).

4. How did the book get its name? The name, *Alcoholics Anonymous,* appears to be a derivative of a "nameless bunch of alcoholics," the term used to describe the New York members of the young fellowship after its break from the Oxford Group in 1937. (*AACA,* 165) Who coined the name remains in dispute, though credit is often given to Joe W., a writer for the *New Yorker.* (*PIO;* 202) A number of titles were suggested for the book, with *The Way Out* favored by a majority of members in Akron, and *Alcoholics Anonymous* supported by most in New York. (*PIO;* 203)   A nod was finally given to *Alcoholics Anonymous* after research in the Library of Congress by Fitz M. ("Our Southern Friend") revealed that twenty-five books were titled *The Way Out,* twelve "The Way," but none, *Alcoholics Anonymous.* (*PIO,* 203)

5. How did *Alcoholics Anonymous* get its nickname? Simple, it was a *big book* – more than a half-inch thicker than the current fourth edition, though it contained thirteen fewer stories and 175 fewer pages. As compensation for its $3.50 price tag (rather hefty in 1939), it was printed on the heaviest stock paper at Cornwall Press. The book was bound in a dark red cloth cover, with gold cursive lettering spelling out the name, *Alcoholics Anonymous.* Subsequent first edition printings – sixteen in all – were bound in various shades of blue, except for the fourth, which was bound in blue and green. (www.barefootsworld.net/aabigbook1939.html) On the rear inside flap of the book's dust jack – the so-called "Circus jacket" for its bright red, gold, yellow and black coloring – were found the following words:

> "This book may be ordered from the publisher upon a free examination basis. Send $3.50 or instruct to send C.O.D. and pay the few extra cents money return cost. Examine for seven days and if not satisfied that the book will be helpful return and money (including postage) will be refunded." (First edition)

6. Where did the idea of a book come from anyway? From talks in 1937 between Bill W. and Dr. Bob on how to best reach the still suffering alcoholic. Explored in these discussions were paid workers or "missionaries"; the operation of a chain of hospitals to treat alcoholics (important as few medical facilities at that time were willing to admit problem drinkers); and a book setting forth the as yet named group's spiritual program of action. (*PIO,* 179-180)

7. Who wrote the Big Book? Primary authorship goes to Bill Wilson, though Chapter 10, "To Employers," may have been written by Hank Parkhurst. (*PIO,* 200) It should be noted, however, that Bill did not write the book alone. Drafts were routinely reviewed by Dr. Bob and other members of the young fellowship, and 400 copies of the manuscript – the Multilith (see study of Chapter 5) – were circulated for final inspection to friends and allies. (Ibid) Too, the Big Book is not merely a distillation of the experience, strength, and hope of AA's early members. Bill – indeed Alcoholics Anonymous as a whole – borrowed generously from the rich reservoir of science, religion, medicine, spirituality, and psychology. From Dr. William Silkworth, Bill learned of alcoholism as an allergy of the body and obsession of the mind (see "The Doctor's Opinion"). Teachings from the Bible and the Oxford Group (especially the words and writings of Sam Shoemaker) are evident in the body and soul of AA's twelve steps or design for living. And American psychologist and philosopher William James' reflections on religious or conversion experiences find expression in the Big Book's discussion of spiritual awakenings (see Appendix II, "Spiritual Experience"). In sum, the text portion of *Alcoholics Anonymous* is more a collaborative or *we* effort than the product of a single spirit.

As for the Personal Stories, sixteen histories were obtained from members in Akron and twelve from New York. (*PIO,* 200) The Stories section has been amended with each later edition (1955, 1976, and 2001) "so that every alcoholic reader may find a reflection of him or herself in it." (Preface, xi)

8. How long did it take to complete the Big Book? Approximately one year: Bill's first notations on yellow scratch sheets date to March or April 1938 (*PIO;* 193), and publication was April 1939.

9. When were the second, third and fourth editions published? The second edition of the Big Book was published in 1955 (16 printings through 1974), the third in 1976 (74 printings through 2001), and the fourth in October 2001.

Memorable Dates

- November 1934 - Ebby Thacher carries a message of hope and recovery to Bill Wilson (the exact day is lost to history).

- December 11, 1934 - Bill W. takes his last drink; enters Towns Hospital. Has conversion experience (spiritual awakening) the second or third day, depending on the source.

- May 12, 1935 (Mother's Day) - Bill W. introduced to Dr. Bob in Akron, Ohio, by fellow Oxford Group member Henrietta Seiberling at Henrietta's residence, the Gatehouse of the Seiberling estate.

- June 10, 1935 - Dr. Bob's last drink; AA born ("Founder's Day"). (Mitchell K., AA historian, has put this date into question. See page 156 of the study guide.)

- September 1935 - Bill returns home from Akron; AA begins in New York City.

- September 1937 - Florence R. becomes the first female member of AA. Her story, "A Feminine Victory," appears in the first edition of *Alcoholics Anonymous*.

- Winter 1937- New York AA members separate from the Oxford Group.

- December 1938 - Twelve Steps were written by Bill W. on a tablet of yellow scratch paper while lying ill in his bed at the Wilson home at 182 Clinton Street, Brooklyn, New York. (*PIO,* 197)

- April 1939 - *Alcoholics Anonymous* published.

- Winter 1939 - Akron AA makes a formal split from Oxford Group. AA is on its own.

- March 1941 - First women's group formed in Cleveland, Ohio

- March 1941 - Jack Alexander article, "Alcoholics Anonymous – Freed Slaves of Drink, Now They Free Others," in *Saturday Evening Post* generates significant public interest in the Fellowship. (*PIO,* 247)

- 1942 - First prison group; San Quentin, California

- June 1944 - First issue of *AA Grapevine* published.

- July 1950 - AA's First International Convention begins in Cleveland Ohio. Twelve traditions formally adopted. Dr. Bob gives his last public talk; Reminds Cleveland audience that it's a simple program, and implores to not "louse it all up with Freudian complexes" and matters unrelated to AA's mission. (*DB,* 338)

- May 1951 - Al-Anon founded by Lois Wilson and Anne B.

- June 1953 - *Twelve Steps and Twelve Traditions* published.

- 1955 - Second edition of *Alcoholics Anonymous* published.

- 1976 - Third edition of *Alcoholics Anonymous* published.

- October 2001 – Fourth edition of *Alcoholics Anonymous* published.

Four Founding Moments in AA's History

The four "founding moments" of AA as cited by Ernest Kurtz in his book, *Not-God* (33), are:

• **1931** - Swiss psychiatrist Carl Jung recommends a religious conversion experience to Rowland Hazard, "a certain American business man" (26-28), as a solution to his obsession with beverage alcohol.

• **November 1934** - Ebby Thacher carries a message of hope and recovery to Bill Wilson (8-13).

• **December 1934** - Bill Wilson has "hot flash" or "white-light experience" in Towns Hospital during third and final treatment (14). Introduced to William James' *The Varieties of Religious Experience*. Reading helps place illumination within the context of conversion or spiritual experience.

• **May to June 1935** - Interaction between Bill W. and Dr. Robert Smith in Akron, Ohio climaxes with Dr. Bob's last drink on June 10; AA is born (Founder's Day).

☞ Synchronicity, a concept coined by Jung that posits meaningful coincidences between acausal events that appear meaningfully connected (Wikipedia) seems to fit the above moments. (Some AAs, however, might read into these moments the unsigned work of a loving Higher Power.)

☞ Note that each of the above moments is founded in a *connection with*. Recovery is rooted in relationships, and the entirety of *Alcoholics Anonymous* is about the building or renewing and repairing of relationships with self, others, community and Higher Power.

,

Big Book Recovery Philosophy

Rarely have I heard anyone say that the Big Book was an *easy read*. To the modern ear, the ear of the cynic, the skeptic, the non-affiliated or non-believer, much in it may seem curiously dated or downright objectionable. Which strikes me as ironic, as I believe the text to have been written in a spirit of accommodation. Thus, from page 19: "Nothing would please us so much as to write a book which would contain no basis for contention or argument." After all, the last thing anyone wanted was to produce a volume that would be tossed aside by the very reader they wished to reach.

This said, I believe there's another reason the book is as much a dust collector as a guide to the perplexed: it's poorly written and edited. It neglects to offer a tidy outline of the fellowship's recovery philosophy, and falls short in its presentation of the two problems central to the alcoholic's unmanageability:

- Problem one: the alcoholic's *lack of power* (45) over alcohol.

- Problem two: the problem of *self*, the root cause of the alcoholic's troubles (62) and the spiritual (vs. mental or physical) dimension of her alcoholism. (See below, Part II).

☞ The text is suggesting that the alcoholic can no more master the problem of *self* by herself than she can her liquor. In both cases, she must *appeal* to – enter into a *relationship* with – some Power greater than herself if she is to "call her soul her own." Visually we have

Problem: Powerlessness	Solution: Power
Over Alcohol Over Problem of Self	Higher Power Higher Power

Parts I and II of this section provide an outline of the two problems; Part III represents the simplest way I know of to illustrate the conversion – the shift in one's spiritual heading – that lies at the center of the steps directed journey.

Part I.
The Problem & The Solution
(See Appendix A.)

The Big Book's recovery philosophy distils down to these vital points (relevant citation included):

1. Your "lack of power" over alcohol is symptomatic of a primary, chronic, and progressive illness:

   "Best of all, I met a kind doctor [William Silkworth, author of two letters that comprise The Doctor's Opinion] who explained that though certainly selfish and foolish, I have been seriously ill, bodily and mentally." (7)

2. Your illness is comprised of three parts:

   Mental - The *obsession of the mind* i.e., the obsession with intoxication   or controlled drinking.

   Physical - The *allergy of the body,* i.e., lack of control over intake once one has started drinking.

   Spiritual - The problem of *self,* i.e., the root of the alcoholic's troubles.

3. At <u>certain</u> times neither willpower nor self-knowledge will defend you against the overpowering desire to drink. At such times, you need a spiritual solution.

   "Once more: The alcoholic at certain times has no effective mental defense against the first drink. Except in a few rare cases, neither he nor any other human being can provide such a defense. His defense must come from a Higher Power." (43).

4. God is the solution.[a] God will remove your obsession – provide a defense against the first drink[b] – if you seek *connection* with God.[c] Thus the "three pertinent ideas" on page 60:

   Our description of the alcoholic, the chapter to the agnostic, and our personal adventures before and after make clear three pertinent ideas:

   (a) That we were alcoholic and could not manage our alcoholism.
   (b) That probably no human power could have relieved our alcoholism.
   (c) That God could and would if He were sought.[d]

☞ Important to keep in mind that is it is *not* God or AA that keeps the alcoholic sober; rather, it is the alcoholic's *relation*ship with God or AA that delivers her to the sober side of life. Connection – whether with fellowship or Higher Power – is the antidote to intoxication.

5. The problem of *self* stands between you and God's grace, i.e., between you and your relationship with a Power greater than yourself.

> "Though our decision [the step three decision to turn our will and our lives over to the care of a Higher Power, or the management of our alcohol problem over to AA] was a vital and crucial step it could have little permanent effect unless at once followed by an effort to face, and be rid of, the things in ourselves which had been blocking us [from entering into relationship with a power greater than ourselves.] 64, Top

6. Seek God's help in removing whatever stands between you and a relationship with God.

> "Relieve me of the bondage of self that I may better do thy will." (See "Third Step Prayer," p. 63.)

> "My Creator, I am now willing that you should have all of me, good and bad. I pray that you now remove from me every single defect of character which stands in the way of my usefulness to you and my fellows. Grant me strength, as I go out from here, to do your bidding." ("Seventh Step Prayer," p. 76)

7. You have but a daily reprieve from the alcohol obsession (i.e., first drink) contingent on the maintenance of your Higher Power relationship.

> "It is easy to let up on the spiritual program of action and rest on our laurels. We are headed for trouble if we do, for alcohol is a subtle foe. We are not cured of alcoholism. What we have is a daily reprieve contingent on the maintenance of our spiritual condition." (85)

8. Continue to seek and do God's will, work the steps, and carry AA's message of recovery to other alcoholics.

In Sum: The Big Book is prescribing a *spiritual* solution to the merciless obsession. That is, a solution rooted in relationship or connection with a Power greater than the alcoholic. (See Appendix I.)

☞ An alternate way of phrasing the solution: Connection is the antidote to intoxication.

---

a. The solution is *not* more willpower to resist addiction's call; the solution is removal of the call itself. See bottom of 84 through top of 85.

b. Remember, it's the *first* drink that's the problem. Stay away from one and there's nothing to seek out the company of two and more.

c. The reader is cautioned against throwing out the Big Book's message of hope and deliverance with a spirituality she may find wanting. Remember: It's *your* Higher Power (or higher power) as you understand It (or it).

d. Possible alternate reading of the last pertinent idea: That connection with AA program and fellowship could and would relieve us of our obsession. (*Step two*)

Part II.
"Bottles Were Only a Symbol"
(See Appendix B.)

1. In the Big Book, the bottle emerges as both symbol and symptom[a] of being (living) out of a relationship with one's God.

    "After all, our problems were of our own making. Bottles were only a symbol." (103)

    "Though our decision ["to turn our will and our lives over to the care of God as we understood Him," or the management of our alcohol problem over to AA] was a vital and crucial step, it could have little permanent effect unless at once followed by a strenuous effort to face, and be rid of, the things in ourselves that had been blocking us [from our Higher Power, or doing our Higher Power's will for us]. Our liquor was but a symptom [of a spiritual ill: not living in relationship with our God]." (64)

2. This waywardness is rooted in the problem of "self" (the philosophy of self-sufficiency).[b]

    "Selfishness – self-centeredness![c] That, we think, is the root of our troubles." (62)

    "So our troubles, we think, are basically of our own making. They arise out of ourselves, and the alcoholic is an extreme example of self-will run riot, though he usually doesn't think so. Above everything, we alcoholic must be rid of this selfishness." (62)

3. As the bottle stands as a symbol or symptom of being out of a relationship with one's God, so the solution to the bottle – the lifting of the merciless obsession – lies in living in relationship with one's God.

    "We had to find a power by which we could live, and it had to be a *Power greater than ourselves.*" (45)

    "Well, that's exactly what this book is about. Its main object is to enable you to find a Power greater than yourself which will solve your problem." (45)

    "We are not cured of alcoholism. What we really have is a daily reprieve contingent on the maintenance of our spiritual condition [or Higher Power relationship]." (85)

    "Remind the prospect that his recovery . . . is dependent upon his relationship with God." (99-100)

    "See to it that your relationship with Him is right, and great events will come to pass for you and countless others." (164)

4. AA's twelve steps help facilitate the building or renewing and sustaining of the prescribed Higher Power relationship.

---

a. The bottle and its attendant suffering and unmanageability come to symbolize a failed spirituality: a life rooted in the philosophy of self-sufficiency (see last paragraph 52, and 60 to 63 in the Big Book, and 36 to the top of 37 in the *12x12*). To illustrate: The process of relapse is most often preceded by a retreat into self-reliance, a *breaking of connection* with one's Higher Power or support system. The reemergence of the bottle symbolizes this falling away from the Spirit or spirit.

b. Alcoholics obviously have no monopoly on "selfishness – self-centeredness." Why then their lot to have the illness of alcoholism? The Big Book suggests the additional factors of physical allergy and acquired mental obsession.

c. Though the text fingers willfulness and egregious pride as the spiritual culprits behind the alcoholic's failed spiritual heading, this need not be the case. As Linda Mercadante notes in her *Victims & Sinners:*

> 'Self-will run riot' is by far not the only way to turn from God." (39) "Sin can be two-sided. One need not sin only through self-elevation; one can sin also through inordinate self-abnegation or denigration, as women have generally been led to do. I have called this 'the sin of self-loss.' One can fall in ungodly despair through refusing to be a full self as much as through defiantly trying to assume Godlike proportion. This sin of sloth can be equally destructive in prompting alienation from God." (*VS,* 149)

Reminder: The Big Book is prescribing a Higher Power relationship as antidote to the spiritual dimension of the alcoholic's problem: "selfishness—self-centeredness (62), as manifested in estrangement from his God. The reader seeking a solution rooted in medicine, psychology, self-knowledge, fitness, nutrition, etc. is simply barking up the wrong book.

Part III.
"It's a Simple Program"

Give Up?
Yes.
Turn to God.

This is the simplest way I know to illustrate the conversion or spiritual shift woven into the steps directed journey: from a life centered around my "little plans and designs" (63) to a life centered around my Higher Power's designs for me; from a life of self-reliance or self-sufficiency to a life of reliance on something or Something. As to the whys of this shift, this new spiritual heading? For some, it may be illness, divorce, war or death – any circumstance that jolts to the core. For the alcoholic, calamity and defeat at the hands of King Alcohol. Again, the "three pertinent ideas" on page 60:

(a) That we were alcoholic and cold not manage our own lives.
(b) That probably no human power could have relieved our alcoholism.
(c) That God could and would if He were sought.[b]

And from Chapter 1, "Bill's Story":

There I humbly offered myself to God, as I then understood Him, to do with me as He would. I placed myself unreservedly under His care and direction. I admitted for the first time that of myself I was nothing; *that without Him I was lost.* (13, Italics added)

And from Psalm 70: "Make *haste*, O God, to deliver me; make haste to help me, O Lord." (*The Holy Bible - Masonic Edition*; A. J. Holman Co., Philadelphia, Pennsylvania. As referenced in *The Spirituality of Imperfection*, 20)

☞ Alcoholics have no monopoly on calamity and defeat, or on reaching beyond their limited resources for help in problem-solving. No wonder the ready acceptance and use of the twelve steps menu by legions of non-alcoholics. Neither Psalm 70 nor the citation from "Bill's Story" make mention of alcohol. Imperfection and essential finiteness is a condition of the being, human. Sadly, many alcoholics only come to this truth after being repeatedly mugged by the bottle.

a.   Remember: It's *your* God or god as *you* understand your God or god. What's important is that: (i) It is not you. (ii) It can help you. (iii) You can form a relationship with it.

b.   Again, the bottle both symbolizes and is symptomatic of the failed spiritual heading of *going-it-aloneness*.

Alcoholics Anonymous

Preface

Summary - Introduces the second edition of the Big Book to the reader. Highlights changes in the course of revisions to the text (almost exclusively related to the appendices and deletion or addition of new stories), and offers rationale for story changes ("to present a more accurate representation of our membership as it is today . . . so that every alcoholic reader may find a reflection of him or herself in it"). Ob "that there exists a sentiment against any radical changes being made" to the book as it "has become the basic text for our Society and has helped such large numbers of alcoholic men and women to recovery." (One such change can be found in the three pertinent ideas on page 60. In the First edition, line (c) reads: "That God could and would if sought." In all three later editions we have: "That God could and would if He were sought.")

Foreword to First Edition

Summary - Provides the primary purpose of the book: "To show other alcoholics *precisely how we have recovered"* from "a seemingly hopeless state of mind and body." (The answer is concisely provided on page 45: We recovered by finding "a power by which we could live . . . a *Power greater than ourselves"* which solved our problem.) Expresses the hope that the text "will prove so convincing that no further authentication will be necessary," i.e., readers will be spared further field research before accepting that they have lost control over their drinking. Stresses the importance of personal anonymity and urges each "of our Fellowship to omit his personal name . . . when writing or speaking publicly about alcoholism." Notes that AA is "not allied with any particular faith, sect or denomination," and that "the only requirement for membership is an honest desire to stop drinking" (third of AA's Twelve Traditions; word "honest" dropped in 1958).

Page xiii
Top. "To show other alcoholics *precisely how we have recovered* is the main purpose of this book." "Recovered" suggests the idea of cure or remission and is often contrasted with "recovering," (i.e., Hello. My name is Dr. Bob and I'm a recovering alcoholic.), which better captures the notion of a chronic or lasting condition. Within the context of the Big Book, however, the difference between these words seems one of style rather than substance.

The book repeatedly notes and stresses the chronic nature of alcoholism: "Once an alcoholic, always an alcoholic." (33); and, "We alcoholics are men and women who have lost the ability to control our drinking. We know that no real alcoholic *ever* recovers control." (30) A suggested reading of recovered is that of obsession lifted or removed. Thus, "To show other alcoholics *precisely how we have recovered . . .*" becomes, "To show other alcoholics precisely [how our obsession to drink was removed] is the main purpose of this book." It must be understood, however, that the lifting of the obsession is no more fixed in time than is the illness ever cured. From page 85: "We are not cured of alcoholism. What we really have is a daily reprieve [from the merciless obsession] contingent on the maintenance of our spiritual condition [or Higher Power relationship]." The notion of daily reprieve is also captured in these fine words from Dr. Bob to Dick S., author of "He Had to Be Shown": "[Dr. Bob] said, 'So long as I'm thinking as I'm thinking now, and so long as I'm doing the things I'm doing now, I don't believe I'll ever take another drink.'" (Second edition, 206-07); and the opening line from Esther E's story, "A Flower Of The South": "I know that if I do daily what I have done for these last thirteen and a half years, I will stay sober." (Second edition, 343)

☞ The alcoholic's *problem* is identified throughout the text as both *lack of power* (powerlessness) over alcohol (45) and *selfishness--self-centeredness.* (62) Thus, "Lack of power, that was our dilemma." And, "Selfishness— self-centeredness! That we think is the root of our troubles." For both problems, the grace of a Higher Power is advanced as a solution. Thus, with powerlessness: "We had to find a power by which we could live, and it had to be a Power greater than ourselves." (45) And with the problem of self: ". . . there often seems no way of entirely getting rid of self without His aid." (62) In short, the text is arguing that alcoholic can no more master the problem of self by herself than she can her liquor. In both cases, she must appeal to some power or Power greater than herself if he is to re-create her life. Visually we have:

Problem: Powerlessness	Solution: Power
Over Alcohol Over Problem of Self	Higher Power Higher Power

Page xiv

Top. "We simply wish to be helpful to those who are afflicted." Thus Tradition Five (Short Form): "Each group has but one primary purpose – to carry its message to the alcoholic who still suffers." (See also AA Preamble for a restatement of our primary purpose.)

Foreword to Second Edition

Summary - Notes the miraculous increase in AA groups and membership that has occurred in the sixteen years since the original Foreword was written. Provides a brief account of AA's beginnings in Akron, Ohio, and recalls the end of the "flying-blind period" with the April 1939 publication of the Big Book (the fellowship's name, Alcoholics Anonymous, was adopted from the book's title). Describes the impact of favorable press on AA (chiefly the 1941 Jack Alexander feature piece, "Alcoholics Anonymous," in the *Saturday Evening Post*), and offers rationale for the Twelve Traditions: as the individual alcoholic needs principles by which she can live, so also "the A.A. groups and A.A. as a whole" need principles by which to survive and function effectively" (see Appendix I). Notes that Alcoholics Anonymous is not a religious organization, and that "alcohol being no respecter of persons, we are an accurate cross section of America" and other countries. Acknowledges AA's limitations in dealing with "the alcohol problem in all its ramifications. Upon therapy for the alcoholic himself, we surely have no monopoly," while also expressing the "hope that all those who have as yet found no answer may begin to find one in the pages of this book."

Page xv
Bot. ". . . New York stockbroker and an Akron physician." Bill Wilson and Dr. Robert Smith.

Page xvi
Top. ". . . following a meeting with an alcoholic friend . . ." Edwin "Ebby" Thacher.

". . . who had been in contact with the Oxford Groups of that day." See above, Cast Of Characters. For a detailed look at this First Century Christian Fellowship, the reader is referred to *What Is The Oxford Group?* published through Hazelden-Pittman Archives Press.

Top. Though [Bill] could not accept all the tenets of the Oxford Group. . . " Many of these principles would later find expression in AA's Twelve Steps (not surprising when one remembers that both *Bill and Dr. Bob got sober in the Oxford Group*). Thus, moral inventory translates into step four (or the fourth *spiritual activity* of AA); confession of personality defects into step five (fifth spiritual activity); restitution to those harmed into steps eight and nine (eighth and ninth activities); helpfulness to others into the twelfth activity; and the necessity of belief in and dependence upon God into steps two, three, six, seven and eleven.

☞ These same tenets also provided the spiritual underpinnings of AA's pre-1939 "Six-Step program." As reconstructed in Earl T's story, "He Sold Himself Short" (Second edition, 292), they were:

1. Complete deflation.
2. Dependence on and guidance from a Higher Power.
3. Moral inventory.
4. Confession
5. Restitution
6. Continued work with other alcoholics

☞ Oxford Group principles and practices that did not find their way into AA included aggressive evangelism, personal publicity, and the "Four Absolutes" (Honesty, Purity, Unselfishness and Love). Heavy-handedness and absolutism tended to alienate the very people AA wished to attract; personal publicity had the undesired effects of ego inflation and associating individual personalities with the Fellowship as a whole. (*AAS,* 50-51).

Mid. "Prior to his journey to Akron. . ." Bill had muscled his way into a proxy fight to wrest control of the National Rubber Machinery Company. (See pages 153-54.)

Mid. "He suddenly realized that in order to save himself he must carry his message to another alcoholic. That alcoholic turned out to be [Dr. Robert Smith]." Exemplifies the Oxford Group's principle, "Giving it away to keep it." (See also pages 14-15, 153-54, and 179-80.)

Page xvii
Top. "Their very first case, a desperate one, recovered immediately and became AA number three." Reference to Bill D., "the man on the bed" (see also pages 156-58, and the story, "Alcoholic Anonymous Number Three.")

☞ In truth, Bill D. was not their first case but their first success. The subject of their initial twelfth-step call was Eddy R. (*PIO,* 151-52)

Top. "When the broker returned to New York in the fall of 1935." August 26, 1935. (*PIO,* 160)

Mid. ". . . there were scattered alcoholics who had picked up the basic ideas in Akron or New York who were trying to form groups in other cities." One such alcoholic was Clarence S., who formed the third AA group in Cleveland in May 1939. Clarence later claimed that this was the first group to call itself Alcoholics Anonymous. (*PIO,* 203)

Page xviii

Mid. "Then Jack Alexander wrote a feature article in the *Saturday Evening Post*. . ." March 1, 1941.

☞ Not all press was as favorable as the Alexander piece. This dismissive remark was noted in the *Journal of the American Medical Association* on October 14, 1939: "This book [Alcoholics Anonymous] is a curious combination of organizing propaganda and religious exhortation . . . The one valid thing in the book is the recognition of the seriousness of addiction to alcohol. Other than this, the book has no scientific merit or interest." (*NG*, 92)

Page xix

Top. ". . . out of this frightening and at first disrupting experience the conviction grew that A.A.'s had to hang together or die separately. We had to unify our Fellowship or pass off the scene." Thus, from Appendix I, "The A.A. Traditions":

> To those now in its fold, Alcoholics Anonymous has made the difference between misery and sobriety, and often the difference between life and death . . . Therefore, no society of men and women ever had a more urgent *need* for continuous effectiveness and permanent unity. We alcoholics see that we must work together and hang together else most of us will finally die alone. (Second edition, 563)

This sentiment is also reflected in Tradition One: "Our common welfare should come first; personal recovery depends upon A.A. unity." (Second edition, 464)

Page xxi

Top. "Upon therapy for the alcoholic himself, we surely have no monopoly." Contrary to the cries of many of its detractors, Alcoholics Anonymous does *not* claim to be the way for every alcoholic. It's simply the way for alcoholics in AA. Thus, from page 95:

> If he thinks he can do the job in some other way, or prefers some other spiritual approach, encourage him to follow his own conscience. We have no monopoly on God; *we merely have an approach that worked with us* [italics added]. But point out that we alcoholics have much in common and that you would like, in any case, to be friendly. Let it go at that. (95)

☞ People new to AA or recovery may well encounter folks in the fellowship who not only claim that AA is the only way, but that the way they themselves do the only way is the sole way to do it. It's important to remember that

Alcoholics Anonymous - book, program, and fellowship - makes no claim that it's the only way out of the bottle or problem or self.

Foreword to Third Edition

Summary – Continues to shine a light on the growth of AA, in particular, the increased number of women, young adults, and teens finding their way into the fellowship. Also, reminds the reader that recovery begins when one alcoholic shares her story with another alcoholic.

☞ This ministering with the "language of the heart" (*LH,* 243) is found throughout the text and is nicely captured in the below lines from "Doctor's Bob Nightmare." Recounting his initial meeting with Bill on May 12, 1935, the good doctor observed:

> The question which might naturally come into your mind would be: 'What did the man [Bill] do or say that was different from what others had done or said?' It must be remembered that I had read a great deal and talked to everyone who knew, or thought they knew anything about the subject of alcoholism. But [Bill] was a man who had experienced many years of frightful drinking, who had had most all the drunkard's experiences known to man, but who had been cured by the very means I had been trying to employ, that is to say the spiritual approach. He gave me information about the subject of alcoholism which was undoubtedly helpful. *Of far more importance was the fact that he was the first living human with whom I had ever talked, who knew what he was talking about in regard to alcoholism from actual experience. In other words, he talked my language.* (180)

"The Doctor's Opinion"

Summary – "The Doctor's Opinion" is comprised of two letters written by William D. Silkworth, Medical Superintendent of Towns Hospital in New York City (1932 - 1945), and early champion of Alcoholics Anonymous. It offers both an endorsement of the plan of recovery outlined in the text (thereby helping to legitimize AA's spiritual program of action), and a restatement of Silkworth's belief in alcoholism as rooted in illness, not badness, weakness or moral deficiency.

Reminder: Pagination for "The Doctor's Opinion" is from the second edition. The third edition maintains the same numbering. "The Doctor's Opinion" begins on page xxv in the fourth edition.

Page xxiii

Top. "Convincing testimony must surely come from medical men who have had experience with the sufferings of our members and have witnessed our return to health." It is estimated that Silkworth ministered to more than 51,000 alcoholics during his career – 45,000 at Towns Hospital and 6,000 at Knickerbocker. (*S,* 194)

☞ Despite Silkworth's championing the idea of alcoholism as an allergy of the body and obsession of the mind ("Best of all, I met a kind Doctor who explained that though certainly selfish and foolish, I had been seriously ill, bodily and mentally" (7)), but scant attention is given the latter idea in "The Doctor's Opinion" – and then but obliquely: "After they have succumbed to the desire again . . . (xxvii)

Reference to the physical *and* mental aspects of the illness can be found in "Dr. Silkworth's Rx for Sobriety." (See Appendix F.)

> Alcoholism is a mental and physical issue. Physically a man has developed an illness. He cannot use alcohol in moderation, at least not for a period of enduring length. If the alcoholic starts to drink, he sooner or later develops the phenomenon of craving. Mentally this same alcoholic develops an obsessive type of thinking which, in itself a neurosis, offers an unfavorable prognosis through former plans of treatment. Physically science does not know why a man cannot drink in moderation. But through moral psychology – a new interpretation of an old idea –AA has been able to solve his former mental obsession. It is the vital principle of A.A., without which A.A. would have failed even as other forms of treatment have failed." (*AA Grapevine,* June 1945. © June 1945 by the AA Grapevine, Inc. Reprinted with permission of AA Grapevine, Inc.)

☞ Silkworth was not the first physician to regard alcoholism as rooted in illness. That distinction appears to belong to Dr. Benjamin Rush (1745-1813), a signer of the Declaration of Independence and Surgeon General of the Continental Army. His "An Inquiry into the Effects of Spirituous Liquors on the Human Body and the Mind" (1784) offered the first articulation of a disease model in the States. It identified alcohol as the addictive agent, loss of control its chief feature, and total abstinence as the sole means of arresting the malady. ("Managing Alcoholism As A Disease," Hobbs, Thomas R., PhD., MD; *Physician's News Digest;* February 1998)

☞ **There is *no* reference to alcoholism as a *disease* in "The Doctor's Opinion" or text portion of the Big Book (1 - 164).** Alcohol use disorder is instead identified as an illness, malady or allergy. (The word disease appears but once, on the bottom of page 64: "From [resentment] stem all forms of spiritual disease . . .")

Responding to a question following his address to the National [Catholic] Clergy Conference on Alcoholism in 1961, Bill observed:

> We have never called alcoholism a disease because, technically speaking, it is not a disease entity. For example, there is no such thing as heart disease. Instead there are many separate heart ailments, or combinations of them. It is something like that with alcoholism. Therefore we did not wish to get in wrong with the medical profession by pronouncing alcoholism a disease entity. Therefore we always called it an illness, or a malady a far safer term for us to use. ("Alcoholics Anonymous and the Disease Concept of Alcoholism"; Kurtz, Ernest, Ph.D.)

☞ **There is *no* reference to alcoholism as a *fault-free illness* in the Big Book.** Alcoholism – at least *Alcoholics Anonymous'* understanding of alcoholism – may be one of numerous ailments for which an individuals bears some responsibility for acquiring. The Big Book argues that the alcoholic's inability to control his or her drinking is rooted in illness – *not* that the alcoholic plays no role in developing this illness. (The reader is invited to mull over the "self-imposed crisis we could not postpone or evade" on page 53, and the italicized paragraph on page 103.)

Top. "A well-known doctor. . ." William Duncan Silkworth, 1871-1951. (*S,* vii)

Top. ". . . a nationally prominent hospital." Founded by Charles B. Towns, Towns Hospital at 293 Central Park West, New York City, "was primarily a place for the wealthy to get back on their feet after a weekend of partying and excessive drinking," at the time Silkworth joined its staff. (*S,* 32) The prescribed treatment, the Towns Cure or Towns-Lambert Treatment (after

Town's associate, Dr. Alexander Lambert), was designed to obliterate the patient's physical craving for alcohol through a rigorous regimen of cathartics (see page 7, the "belladonna treatment"). Total abstinence was stressed as the only way to prevent a relapse into active alcoholism. While the cure itself "appears to border on quackery" (*AAWB,* 87), Towns did come to champion the work of the young fellowship of nameless alcoholics, loaning $2,500 toward the Big Book project at a time when financial backing was in short supply.

☞ Silkworth's arrival at Towns in 1929 was both a godsend to the hospital (it's "cure" was being questioned and referrals were drying up) and alcoholics themselves:

> ". . . Towns needed a new direction in treatment and validity and respect for their alcoholic detoxification program. . .
>
> Silkworth literally reinvented the treatment model at Towns Hospital. He worked personally and closely with every patient. He set up an around-the-clock staffing of nurses, where they had once worked only a normal day shift on the ward. He grew to know the alcoholic and, like no other, gained greater insight into the alcoholic mind.
>
> Before Silkworth arrived . . . the hospital treatment model –the once-famous Towns-Lambert Treatment – focused on a medicinal curing of the physical body. Yet Silkworth found that the physical remedy only opened the mind to a spiritual level of recovery necessary for continuous sobriety. . . Silkworth combined counseling, therapy, psychiatry, and spirituality work with the physical treatment. He began a program of hospital rest and nutrition, medication, and counseling. No longer were the patients allowed to leave without being taught that alcoholism was both a physical allergy and a compulsion to drink." (*Silkworth - The Little Doctor Who Loved Drunks,* by Dale Mitchel. © 2002 by Hazelden Foundation. Reprinted by permission of Hazelden Foundation. Page 33)

Mid. "In late 1934 I attended a patient who . . ." Bill Wilson

Mid. "In the course of his third [and final] treatment . . ." December 11-18, 1934. Fee: $125.00

". . . he acquired certain ideas concerning a possible means of recovery." The "certain ideas" included tenets from the Oxford Group and William James' teachings on conversion (see below, "psychic change"). Oxford group principles were "the need for moral inventory, confession of personality defects, restitution to those harmed, helpfulness to others, and the necessity of belief in and dependence upon God" (Foreword to Second Edition, xvi)

Bot. "As part of his rehabilitation he commenced to present his conceptions to other alcoholics . . ." From page 14, bottom:

> "My friend [Ebby] had emphasized the absolute necessity of demonstrating these principles in all my affairs. Particularly was it imperative to work with others as he had worked with me. Faith without works was dead, he said. And how appallingly true for the alcoholic! For if an alcoholic failed to perfect and enlarge his spiritual life through work and self-sacrifice for others, he could not survive the certain trials and low spots ahead."

☞ One of the "low spots ahead" was Bill's involvement in an unsuccessful proxy fight to gain control of the National Rubber Machinery Company in Akron, Ohio, in May 1935:

> "Years ago . . . one of our number made a journey to a certain western city. From a business standpoint, his trip came off badly. Had he been successful in his enterprise, he would have been set on his feet financially which, at the time, seemed vitally important. But his venture wound up in a law suit and bogged down completely . . .
>
> Bitterly discouraged, [Bill] found himself in a strange place, discredited and almost broke. Still physically weak, and sober but a few months, he saw that his predicament was dangerous. He wanted so much to talk with someone, but whom?" [That someone turned out to be fellow Oxford Group member, Dr. Robert Smith.] (153-54)

Page xxiv
Top. ". . . they may mark a new epoch in the annals of alcoholism." Realization of this hope reflected in Appendix IV of text:

> "The American Public Health Association presents a Lasker Group Award for 1951 to Alcoholics Anonymous in recognition of its unique and highly successful approach to that age-old public health and social problem, alcoholism . . .In emphasizing alcoholism as an illness, the social stigma associated with this condition is being blotted out . . .Historians may one day recognize Alcoholics Anonymous to have been a great venture in social pioneering which forged a new instrument for social action; a new therapy based on the kinship of common suffering; one having a vast potential for the myriad other ills of mankind."

Mid. ". . . that the body of the alcoholic is quite as abnormal as his mind." A summary statement of these two concepts – *allergy* of the body and *obsession* of the mind – is found on page 44:

> "We hope we have made clear the distinction between the alcoholic and the non-alcoholic. If, when you honestly want to, you find you cannot quite entirely [obsession of the mind], or if when drinking, you have little control over the amount you take [allergy of the body], you are probably alcoholic."

☞ Allergy and obsession are also loaded into the first half of step one. Thus, "We admitted we were powerless over alcohol. . ." may be understood: We admitted that once we started to drink we had little control over the amount we drank (allergy), and we admitted that when we honestly wanted to or tried, we could not entirely keep away from the first drink (obsession).

Page xxv

Mid. "We doctors have realized for a long time that some form of moral psychology was of urgent importance to alcoholics . . ." The term moral psychology was used by Silkworth to characterize the work being done by Bill and other members of the New York Fellowship. (*PIO,* 201) *The* spiritual dimension of this work is partially captured in these lines from Jim B's story, "The Vicious Cycle":

> "At that time the group in New York was composed of about twelve men who were working on the principle of every drunk for himself; we had no real formula and no name. We would follow one's man's ideas for a while, decide he was wrong, and switch to another's method. But we *were* staying sober as long as we kept and talked together. There was one meeting a week at Bill's home in Brooklyn, and we all took turns there spouting off about how we had changed our lives overnight, how many drunks we had saved and straightened out, *and last but not least, how God had touched each of us personally on the shoulder.* Boy, what a circle of confused idealists! Yet we all had one really sincere purpose in our hearts, and that was not to drink." (Second edition, 246. Italics added.)

☞ These two spiritual themes – one alcoholic needing another, and "God [or the AA group] . . . doing for us what we could not do for ourselves" (25) – reverberate throughout the text, and find joint expression in these words from Silkworth himself:

> "The unselfishness of these men as we have come to know them, the entire absence of profit motive, and their community spirit, is indeed inspiring to one who has labored long and wearily in this

alcoholic field. *They believe in themselves, and still more in the Power which pulls chronic alcoholics back from the gates of death."* (xxv) (Italics added.)

And again from "Dr. Silkworth's Rx for Sobriety":

"But through moral psychology – a new interpretation of an old idea – A.A. has been able to solve [an individual's] mental obsession. It is the vital principle of A.A. without which A.A. would have failed even as other forms of treatment have failed.

To be sure, A.A. offers a number of highly useful tools or props. Its group therapy is very effective. I have seen countless demonstrations of how well your '24-hour plan' operates. The principle of working with other alcoholics has a sound psychological basis. All of these features of the program are extremely important.

But, in my opinion, the key principle which makes A.A. work where others plans have proved inadequate is the way of life it proposes based upon the belief of the individual in a Power greater than himself and faith that this Power is all-sufficient to destroy the obsession which possessed him and was destroying him mentally and physically." (*AA Grapevine*, June 1945. © June 1945 by the AA Grapevine, Inc. Reprinted with permission of the AA Grapevine, Inc.)

Thus, from page 25, mid-paragraph:

"The central fact of our lives today is the absolute certainty that our Creator has entered into our hearts and lives in a way which is indeed miraculous. He has commenced to accomplish those things for us which we could never do by ourselves." (A restatement of step two.)

Mid. "What with our ultra-modern standards, our scientific approach to everything, we are perhaps not well equipped to apply the powers of good that lie outside our synthetic knowledge." Silkworth admits to the limits of his art. The same courageous concession is also made by Carl Jung to his patient, Rowland Hazard (see First Founding Moment in AA): science and western medicine cannot liberate you from the bottle (26-27). Only through a Higher Power relationship – through moral psychology – might you harness the "powers of good" that will deliver you from the merciless obsession.

Mid. ". . . one of the leading contributors to this book. . ." Bill Wilson

Bot. "Later, [Bill] requested the privilege of being allowed to tell his story to other patients here and with some misgiving, we consented." Amongst those other patients were Hank P., whose story, "The Unbeliever," appeared in the first edition and John Henry "Fitz" M. "Our Southern Friend."

Bot. "The unselfishness of these men as we have come to know them. . . They believe in themselves, and still more in the Power which pulls chronic alcoholics back from the gates of death." Moral psychology or application of the "powers of good." See above citation from "The Vicious Cycle."

Page xxvi
Top. We believe, and so suggested a few years ago, that the action of alcohol on these chronic alcoholics is a manifestation of an allergy. . ." From "Alcoholism As A Manifestation Of Allergy":

> . . . true alcoholism is an allergic state, the result of gradually increasing sensitization by alcohol over a more or less extended period of time. The constancy of the symptoms and progress is too fixed to permit any other explanation. Some are allergic from birth, but the condition usually develops later in life. The development and course of these cases are quite comparable with the history of hay fever patients, in many respects. One may enjoy absolute freedom for many years from any susceptibility to pollen. Year after year, however, there gradually develops a sensitivity to it in certain individuals, culminating at last in paroxysms of hay fever that persist indefinitely when the condition is fully established.
>
> It is noteworthy also, that such patients may be deprived of liquor altogether for a long period, a year or longer for example, and become apparently normal. They are still allergic, however, and a single drink will develop the full symptomatology again. (Silkworth, W.D.; *Medical Record;* March 17, 1937, 249-51)

☞ Silkworth may have used the term allergy more as metaphor or analogy (e.g., to hay fever) than as scientific fact:

> Yet its core meaning lives on and is finding favor once again in modern-day research. One dictionary defines allergy as "a hypersensitivity to a specific substance or condition which in similar amounts is harmless to most people. It is manifested by a physical disorder. A strong disorder." Alcoholics have just such a reaction to alcohol. Many social drinkers consume alcohol in similar amounts to active alcoholics without any life problems at all. (*S*, 57)

"Only recently has brain chemistry analysis – neurotransmitters, such as serotonin, and brain receptors – come into the mainstream of alcoholism research. Research has once again turned to the physical manifestations of an allergic type of long-term reaction to alcohol within the alcoholic physiology. For years, researchers have flavored the results of scientific studies with reference to a physiological difference in the alcoholic brain. For even longer, scientists have known alcoholics metabolize alcohol differently than non-alcoholics. A physical disorder is simply an upset in the normal function of a physiological system. It is an irregularity. What else could we call alcoholism?" (*Ibid,* 59)

Top. ". . . and once having formed the habit and found they cannot break it . . ." Suggested reading: once having lost control of their drinking and found they cannot regain it. (See above citation from *Medical Record*.)

". . . their problems pile up on them and become astonishingly difficult to solve." Step one: "We admitted we were powerless over alcohol – *that our lives had become unmanageable.*" (Italics added.)

Mid. "Frothy emotional appeal seldom suffices. The message which can interest and hold these alcoholic people must have depth and weight. In nearly all cases, their ideals must be grounded in a power greater than themselves, if they are to re-create their lives." Suggested reading: The pleas and pleadings of family and friends, employers and physicians, rarely suffice in separating "these alcoholic people" from the bottle. In nearly all cases their "defense must come from a Higher Power [relationship]." (43)

Mid. "If any feel that as psychiatrists directing a hospital for alcoholics we appear somewhat sentimental, let them stand with us a while on the firing line. . . and the most cynical will not wonder that we have accepted and encouraged this [altruistic] movement [of a nameless bunch of alcoholics]." In the early years of his work at Towns, the recovery rate for alcoholics was less than two percent. Fatality rates from late stage delirium tremens were also very high. (*S,* 34-35)

Bot. "Men and women drink essentially because they like the effect produced by alcohol." Obsession of the mind (obsession with the experience of intoxication). See also page 152, top:

"He cannot picture life without alcohol. Some day he will be unable to imagine life either with alcohol or without it. Then he will know loneliness such as few do. He will be at the jumping-off place. He will wish for the end."

Page xxvii
Top. "After they have succumbed to the desire again. . ." Obsession of the mind.

". . . and the phenomenon of craving develops. . ." Allergy of the body.

Top. ". . .once a psychic change has occurred. . ." Psychic change may require some explanation. Helpful to an understanding of this concept is the following:

(1) Psychic change is generally known in the text as a spiritual awakening or spiritual experience. It is this very spiritual experience or "personality change sufficient to bring about recovery from alcoholism" (Appendix II, top) that Jung prescribes for Rowland Hazard, and that Rowland later finds through his involvement with the Oxford Group (First Founding Moment in AA history). As attributed to Jung on page 27:

> ". . . once in a while, alcoholics have had what are called vital spiritual experiences. To me these occurrences are phenomenon. They appear to be in the nature of huge emotional displacements and rearrangements. Ideas, emotions, and attitudes which were once the guiding forces of [their lives] are suddenly cast to one side, and a completely new set of conceptions and motives begin to dominate [them]."

To illustrate:

> ". . . fear changes into faith, hate into love, egoism into humility, anxiety and worry into serenity, complacency into action, denial into acceptance, jealousy into trust, fantasizing into reality, selfishness into service, resentment into forgiveness, judgmentalism into tolerance, despair into hope, self-hate into self-respect, and loneliness into fellowship." (*PTP,* xi-xii)

> "This last part of my life has had a purpose, not in great things accomplished but in daily living. Courage to face each day has replaced the fears and uncertainties of earlier years. Acceptance of things as they are has replaced the old impatient chomping at the bit to change the world. I have stopped tilting at windmills, and instead have tried to accomplish the little daily tasks, unimportant in themselves, but tasks that are an integral part of living fully." ("He Sold Himself Short," Second edition, 295)

> "A complete change takes place in our approach to life. Where we used to run from responsibility, we find ourselves accepting it with gratitude that we can successfully shoulder it. Instead of wanting

to escape some perplexing problem, we experience a thrill of challenge in the opportunity it affords for another application of A.A. techniques, and we find ourselves tackling it with surprising vigor." ("The Keys of the Kingdom," Second edition, 311-12)

(2) Such personality changes are the substance of William James' lectures on conversion in his *The Varieties of Religious Experience* (see above, Third Founding Moment):

> "To be converted, to be regenerated, to receive grace, to experience religion, to gain an assurance, are so many phrases which denote the process, gradual or sudden, by which a self hitherto divided, and consciously wrong inferior and unhappy, becomes unified and consciously right superior and happy, in consequence of its firmer hold upon religious realities. This at least is what conversion signifies in general terms. . ." (*VRE,* 189)

James did not, however, believe that "direct divine operation is needed to bring such a moral change about," (Ibid, 189) and indeed argued that the value of any such conversion or personality change must be decided solely on empirical grounds, that is, outcome – not origin:

> "If the *fruits for life* of the state of conversion are good, we ought to idealize and venerate it, even though it be a piece of natural psychology; if not, we ought to make short work with it, no matter what supernatural being may have infused it." (Ibid, 237)

For instance, Bill W's awakening or white light experience in Towns Hospital is no less significant if rooted in alcohol-induced psychosis (as skeptics have argued) than the divine. What shines is the positive attained for Bill – he never took another drink, he never again doubted the existence of God (*PIO, 121)* – and through him, millions of others.

(3) Most individuals do *not* enjoy the sudden, dramatic type of transformation experienced by Bill in Towns (or Fitz M. (56), or the apostle Paul on his journey to Damascus). "Most of our experiences are what. . . James calls the 'educational variety' because they develop slowly over a period of time. Quite often friends of the newcomer are aware of the difference long before he is himself." (Appendix II.) Indeed, it was to correct "the impression that these personality changes, or religious experiences, must be in the nature of sudden and spectacular upheavals" (Ibid) that Appendix II was added to the second printing of the first edition.

(4) Psychic or personality changes do not happen in a vacuum, *but within the context* of the individual's *relationships* with others, community, and Higher Power:

"He finally realizes that he has undergone a profound alteration in his reaction to life; that such a change could hardly have been brought about by himself alone. What often takes place in a few months could seldom have been accomplished by years of self discipline." (Ibid)

Put another way, the spiritual changes one begins to realize in the infancy of recovery are not the ends of self-will or self-knowledge, but the fruits of relating oneself rightly with the world. Were this otherwise, there would be little cause for peer-centered treatment, or mutual support groups such as AA, NA, etc.

(5) Spiritual or conversion experiences are not generally the stuff of bouncy hayrides on sunny, summer days. Despite their varied manifestations, Bill's reading of *The Varieties* suggested three common characteristics (*PIO,* 124):

> *Calamity* - each person has confronted defeat in some key area of her life;
> *Admission of defeat* - each person has confronted the limits of her power; and
> *Appeal to a Higher Power* - for solution to her problem.

These elements later find expression in the "three pertinent ideas" on page 60 (*NW,* 24):

(a) That we were alcoholic and could not manage our own lives.
(b) That probably no human power could have relieved our alcoholism.
(c) That God could and would if He were sought.

They are also etched into these wonderful lines from page 50, bottom:

> "In the face of collapse and despair, in the face of the total failure of their human resources, they found that a new power, peace, happiness, and sense of direction flowed into them. This happened soon after they wholeheartedly met a few simple requirements."

☞ Despite the text's assurance that awakenings need not "be in the nature of sudden and spectacular upheavals" (Appendix II), many persist in discounting or ignoring their own spiritually loaded moments out of the mistaken belief that genuine illuminations must be heralded by French horns or hip-hopping angels. Here's something that happened to me (discounted, too, for too many years):

> I didn't understand the stuff of treatment: why the groups, or the lectures, or the assignments; why the getting up at a particular time

or the going to bed at a particular time – or really any of the many things they asked (made) us do.

But I did understand that before treatment I was sitting on a window ledge, one hand holding on tight, the other holding tight to a bottle. And I also understood that for the first time in over ten years I had just gone a whole day without a drink, and then another whole day without a drug, and then a third and a fourth and a fifth day without using as well. And this blew me away (as we said in those days). Cause I was a loser. Yet here I was – not using but winning.

And I began to wonder: might growing up (cause for me not drinking or drugging was always about growing up) be mine at long last? Might Someone be offering me a way out of existence as I had come to know it: of watching the world go by without me, of seeing my friends grow up around me? Of just living to use, and using to live?*

So, I made a quiet decision to begin doing things I was being asked to do. Whether they made sense to me or not. To be honest, it really wasn't all that difficult: by the time my butt hit the treatment door I was ripe for the pickings. The fight was gone. The "hopelessness and futility of life as I had been living it" was obvious to see (sitting on a window ledge will do that to you).

How had I been living it? My way. No one told me what to do. No one knew more, or better, or could best me in an argument, or convince me of the merits of their way or another's. No one that is but the bottle. It convinced me of its way whenever it wanted.

So, as I said, I began doing things I didn't want to do. Things that made little sense, that seemed silly or pointless or downright stupid; uncomfortable things, and foreign things, and things not manly or for children only; and things, I hesitate to say, that only started to make sense many months – or even some years – later.

And on my one year anniversary, as I stood before a gathering of kind, I thanked myself for not self-destructing, and for finally allowing others to help me do what I obviously could not do alone: stay off the ledge.

* *NS,* Fifth Ed., p. 3

Mid. "On the other hand . . . once a psychic change has occurred, the very same person who seemed doomed. . .suddenly finds himself easily able to control his desire for alcohol the only effort necessary being that required to follow a few simple rules." Suggested reading: "On the other hand . . . once [a personality change begins], the very same person who seemed doomed . . . finds [the obsession with intoxication lifted], the only effort necessary being that [she be willing to live in relationship with her Higher Power/work the AA program]." The reader is also directed to this serving of hope on page 85:

> "We are not fighting [liquor], neither are we avoiding temptation. We feel as though we had been placed in a position of neutrality – safe and protected. We have not even sworn off. Instead, the [obsession] has been removed. It does not exist for us. We are neither cocky nor are we afraid. That is our experience. That is how we react so long as we keep in fit spiritual condition."

Mid. "One feels that something more than human power is needed to produce the essential psychic change." A spiritual experience or personality change need not be rooted in religion or belief in the Judeo-Christian God. Quality sobriety is neither synonymous with, nor contingent upon, belief or religious devotion, and many a non-religious individual has been able to realize long-term abstinence through AA alone. What does seem of vital importance, however, is a turning to, a humble reliance on, some *power* greater than oneself. Thus, if we amend or secularize the "three pertinent ideas" on page 60, we have something like:

(a) We were alcoholic and our lives had become unmanageable.
(b) We could not defend ourselves against the first drink.
(c) The AA fellowship could help defend us if we appealed to it for help.

☞ The use of the group as Higher Power – the method of substitution – is cited on page 27 in the *12x12*, and illustrated in Jim Burwell's story, "The Vicious Cycle:"

> For a long time the only Higher Power I could concede was the power of the group, but this was far more than I had ever recognized before, and it was at least a beginning. It was also an ending, for never since June 16, 1938, have I had to walk alone. (Second edition, 248)

Page xxviii
Top. "The classification of alcoholics seems most difficult, and in much detail is outside the scope of this book." I'm equally willing to put this matter outside the guide as well. The issue of alcoholics with pre- or co-existing mental health concerns will be touched upon in the study of Chapter 5, first paragraph. Readers interested in some of the literature on types are referred

to "Typology: The Classification of Alcoholism," in *Alcohol Health & Research World;* National Institute on Alcohol Abuse and Alcoholism; Vol. 20, No. 1, 1996. And the National Institute of Health website of Thursday, June 27, 2008, headlines, "Researchers Identify Alcoholism Subtypes." (https://www.nih.gov/news-events/news-releases/researchers-identify-alcoholism-subtypes)

Page xxix
Top. "About one year prior to this experience a man was brought in to be treated for chronic alcoholism." A likely reference to Hank Parkhurst, whose story, "The Unbeliever," appeared in the first edition. Hank was the first person Bill succeeded in sobering up after his return from Akron to figure in the Big Book's publication. He returned to drinking in 1939 or 1940. (www.silkworth.net/aabiography/hankp.html)

Bot. "His alcoholic problem was so complex, and his depression so great, that we felt his only hope would be through what we then called 'moral psychology'. . . Again, attacking the spirits with the Spirit.

Page xxx
Top. "I earnestly advise every alcoholic to read this book through, and though perhaps he came to scoff, he may remain to pray." This shift – from scoffing or mocking to embracing – is itself a manifestation of spiritual change.

Chapter 1

Bill's Story

Summary - Provides the reader or practicing alcoholic with two things: *identification* - identification with a common problem and a common sufferer (Bill Wilson, co-founder of Alcoholics Anonymous); and *hope* - hope in the form of a success story, the story of one man's triumph over the bottle. (*BBD,* Tape 1, side 2) Instructive is the deflation of Bill's pride and vanity before the god alcohol. Paradoxically, it is this humbling of self in the presence of powerlessness, this whittling down of puffed ego, this forced confrontation with his essential finiteness, that ultimately allows Bill to embrace a spiritual (non-intellectual) remedy to his alcohol problem. To borrow from page 25, second paragraph:

> Almost none of us liked the self-searching, the leveling of our pride, the confession of shortcomings which the process requires for its successful consummation. But we saw that it really worked in others, and we had come to believe in the hopelessness and futility of life as we had been living it. When, therefore, we were approached by those in whom the problem had been solved, there was nothing left for us but to pick up the simple kit of spiritual tools laid at our feet.

Page 1
Top. "War fever ran high..." World War I. Bill received a commission as a second lieutenant in the Army's 66th Coast Artillery Corps. (*LR,* 21)

Top. "I was part of life at last, in the midst of the excitement I discovered liquor. I forgot the strong warnings and the prejudices of my people for drink." At age 21, while stationed at Fort Rodman in New Bedford, Massachusetts, Bill is introduced to alcohol.

☞ Bill had his first drink, a Bronx cocktail (gin, dry and sweet vermouth, and orange juice), while attending a party given by one of New Bedford's leading families. (*PIO,* 56) This was his first time out in society, and he found himself marooned in a sea of fear and ineptitude. In his own words:

> The warnings of my people, the contempt which I had felt for those who drank, were put aside with surprising alacrity as I discovered what the Bronx cocktail could really do for a fellow. My imagination soared – my tongue loosened at last – wonderful vistas opened on all sides, but best of all my self consciousness [sic] – my gaucheries and my ineptitudes disappeared into thin air." (Transcript of Bill Wilson's Original Story; lines 189-195, www.aapubliccontroversy.com/manu/billorig.htm)

Few can turn the back on such experiences. Little wonder, then, that many consider themselves alcoholic from their first date with the bottle. Observes James in *The Varieties:*

> The sway of alcohol over mankind is unquestionably due to its power to stimulate the mystical faculties of human nature, usually crushed to earth by the cold facts and dry criticism of the sober hour. Sobriety diminishes, discriminates, and says no; drunkenness expands, unites, and says yes. It is, in fact, the great exciter of the *Yes* function in man. It brings its votary from the chill periphery of things to the radiant core. It makes him for the moment one with truth. Not through mere perversity do men run after it. To the poor and the unlettered it stands in the place of symphony concerts and of literature; and it is part of the deeper mystery and tragedy of life that whiffs and gleams of something that we immediately recognize as excellent should be vouchsafed to so many of us only in the fleeting earlier phases of what in its totality is so degrading a poison. (387)

☞ For a bit more compelling account of Bill's initial encounter with the spirits, see *Pass It On – Bill Wilson and the A.A. Message,* page 56.)

☞ In January 1961, Bill posted a letter of gratitude to Carl Jung for his unique contribution to AA's founding: prescribing a spiritual remedy for Rowland Hazard's alcohol problem. (See Four Founding Moments In AA History, and pages 26-28 in the Big Book.) Jung's reply letter of January 30 suggested a spiritual or religious dimension to Roland's problem: "His craving for alcohol was the equivalent on a low level of the spiritual thirst of our being for wholeness, expressed in medieval language: the union with God." (*PIO,* 384) A similar notion is found in Craig Nakken's *The Addictive Personality,* where "the out of control and aimless searching for wholeness, happiness, and peace through a relationship with an object or event" (4) is cited as the shared denominator of all addictions and addictive processes. (In later years Bill reportedly shared with at least one audience, "We alcoholics were looking for the spirit, but we went to the wrong address." *TP,* xv)

☞ The reader is invited to consider the similarities in Bill's account of his initial experience with intoxication (awakening to alcohol) and his conversion experience (awakening to God) in Towns Hospital. (See study of page 14.)

Mid. "Much moved, I wandered outside." A veiled reference to a spiritual experience. Stationed outside Winchester, England, lonely, fearful and depressed (*LR,* 25), Bill set out one day to tour the city and its famous Cathedral:

> . . . the moment he stepped into the cool hush of the cathedral, all such thoughts [about the war or where he's be sent], indeed any kind of conscious thinking, seemed to be taken from him. He

moved slowly up the great main aisle, then, halfway to the altar, he paused. His head went back and he stood transfixed, legs spread, gazing up at a shaft of pure light streaming in from the uppermost point of a stained-glass window, absorbing the total silence around him, which seemed part of some vast universal silence, and all his being yearned to go on to become a part of that silence. Then, hardly knowing he was doing it, he moved into a pew and sat, his hands resting on his knees.

How long he sat or what happened or even what state of consciousness he was in he did not know, but he was aware for the first time in his life of a tremendous sense of Presence, and he was completely at ease, completely at peace . . . he understood that all was good and that evil existed only in the mind – and he knew that now, for these fleeting moments, he had moved into some area beyond thought. (*Bill W.*, 106-107)

☞ Troubled and alone, Bill does not find a solution in a book, movie, or companion; nor does willpower or self-knowledge offer rescue from the dark. Rather he realizes (if only momentarily) a stilling of his troubled soul in the presence of his God. If we translate Bill's awakening into the Big Book's conversion template – the three pertinent ideas on page 60 – we have:

(a) Bill admitted to being lonely, depressed, and apprehensive about the future. (*Step One*)
(b) Bill could not help himself. (*Step One*)
(c) God could and would help Bill if He were sought. (*Step Two*)

Bill's illumination was in due course snuffed out by his own ego, vainglory, and drive for success: "My talent for leadership, I imagined, would place me at the head of vast enterprises which I would manage with the utmost assurance." (1) Still, his momentary transformation does highlight use of the steps menu for problems other than alcohol, and the already mentioned problem of self (here masquerading as pride and vanity) as obstacle to conscious contact with one's Higher Power. Thus, from page 12:

The real significance of my experience in the Cathedral burst upon me. For a brief moment, I had needed and wanted God. There had been a humble willingness to have Him with me—and he came. But soon the sense of His presence had been blotted out by worldly clamors, mostly those within myself. And so it had been ever since.

Need would again turn Bill to a Power greater than himself – this time with more permanent and profound results – during has last treatment at Towns.

Mid. "My attention was caught by a doggerel on an old tombstone." The gravestone of Thomas Thetcher, a grenadier in the North Regiment of Hants Militia. The word "pot" refers to an alcoholic drink. (Wikipedia)

Bot. "My talent for leadership, I imagined, would place me at the head of vast enterprises which I would manage with the utmost assurance." Quite the delicious irony: little could Bill imagine that this vast enterprise would turn out to be Alcoholics Anonymous.

Page 2

Top. "Potential alcoholic that I was, I nearly failed my law courses." Bill graduated from Brooklyn Law School in 1924. Liquor did, apparently, kept him from obtaining his diploma the day after he paid for it. He never did get it. (*LR,* 31)

Top. "We had long talks when I would still her foreboding. . ." Wed January 24, 1918, the Wilson marriage was already troubled by Bill's drinking by the early 1920s. (*PIO,* 67)

Bot. "I failed to persuade my broker friends to send me out looking over factories and managements, but [Lois] and I decided to go anyway. I had developed a theory that most people lost money in stocks through ignorance of markets." Bill may have been one of the first securities analysts.

Bot. "We gave up our positions and off we roared on a motorcycle, the sidecar stuffed with tent, blanket, a change of clothes, and three huge volumes of a financial reference service [*Moody's Manuals*]." (*PIO,* 69) Reference to Bill's and Lois's tour of the eastern United States, April 1925 until roughly June 1926. Bill was interested in analyzing the real value of various securities; Lois in controlling his drinking:

> I wanted to get away, too, but my reasons were different. I was so concerned about Bill's drinking that I wanted to get him away from New York and its bars. I felt sure that during a year in the open I would be able to straighten him out. (*LR,* 37)

☞ A photo of Bill, Lois and their Harley-Davidson (a model J or JD) can be found in *Pass It On.*

Page 4

Mid. "I was staring at an inch of the tape which bore the inscription XYZ-32. It had been 52 that morning." Reference to Penick and Ford, a corn products company heavily invested in by Bill and some of his trusting friends. (*PIO,* 85-86)

Bot. ". . . I telephoned a friend in Montreal." Dick Johnson

Bot. "I felt like Napoleon returning from Elba. No St. Helena for me!" Napoleon returned to power after escaping exile to the island of Elba off the west coast of Italy. Defeated at the battle of Waterloo in 1815, he was again exiled – this time permanently – to the island of St. Helena in the South Atlantic Ocean. (*CEO*)

Bot. "We went to live with my wife's parents." Dr. Clark and Matilda Spelman Burnham at 182 Clinton Street, Brooklyn, New York.

Page 5

Top. "Liquor ceased to be a luxury; it became a necessity." Addiction, straight up. An equally compelling (or chilling) picture of addiction is found in Nancy F.'s story, "The Independent Blond": "I had been drunk for nine days, sick and alone and desperate. They didn't have to tell me that alcoholism was a sickness. When you take a bottle and lock that door and go in by yourself, that is death." (Second edition, 535)

Top. "'Bathtub' gin, two bottles a day, and often three, got to be routine." Gin was popular during the prohibition era, 1920 to 1933, as it didn't require aging, and could easily be made at home by combining raw alcohol, juniper berry extract and other flavorings and spices in a large container – like a bathtub. (www.tastings.com/spririts/gin.html)

Bot. "There had been no fight. Where had been my high resolve? I simply didn't know. It hadn't even come to mind. Someone had pushed a drink my way, and I had taken it." Step one powerlessness:

> *The fact is that most alcoholics, for reasons yet obscure, have lost the power of choice in drink. Our so-called will power becomes practically nonexistent. We are unable, at certain times, to bring into our consciousness with sufficient force the memory of the suffering and humiliation of even a week or a month ago. We are without defense against the first drink.* (24)

☞ See also Fred's story, beginning page 39. Story intended to help sell the alcoholic on the need for a Higher Power relationship as defense against the first drink.

Page 7

Top. "My brother-in-law [Dr. Leonard Strong Jr.] is a physician, and through his kindness and that of my mother I was placed in a nationally-known hospital for the mental and physical re-rehabilitation of alcoholics." Bill's first treatment at Towns Hospital in autumn of 1933. (*PIO*, 100) Dr. Strong remained a close friend of Bill's, and later became a nonalcoholic member of the AA Board of Trustees.

Top. "Under the so-called belladonna treatment. . ." The belladonna, Towns Cure, or Towns-Lambert Treatment (after Towns associate, Alexander Lambert, MD), was designed to eliminate the patient's physical craving for beverage alcohol. It

> consists in the hourly dosage of a mixture of belladonna, hyoscyamus, and zanthoxylum. The mixture is given every hour, day and night, for about fifty hours. There is also given about every twelve hours a vigorous catharsis of C.C. pills and blue

mass. At the end of the treatment, when it is evident that there are abundant bilious stools, castor oil is given to clean out thoroughly the intestinal tract. If you leave any of the ingredients out, the reaction of the cessation of desire is not as clear cut as when the three are mixed together. The amount of necessary to give is judged by the physiologic action of the belladonna it contains. When the face becomes flushed, the throat dry, and the pupils of the eyes dilated, you must cut down your mixture or cease giving it altogether until these symptoms pass. You must, however, push this mixture until these symptoms appear, or you will not obtain a clear cut cessation of the desire for [alcohol]. (*S, 32-33*)

Top. Best of all, I met [Dr. Silkworth] who explained that though certainly selfish and foolish, I had been seriously ill, bodily and mentally." Bill's initial exposure to the idea of alcoholism as rooted in illness – not weakness or badness. Additional impact statement can be found in Marty Mann's story, "Women Suffer Too":

That was the point at which my doctor [Dr. Harry Tiebout] gave me the book, "Alcoholic Anonymous" to read. The first chapters were a revelation to me. I wasn't the only person in the world who felt and behaved like this! I wasn't mad or vicious – I was a sick person. I was suffering from an actual disease that had a name and symptoms like diabetes or cancer or TB – and a disease was respectable, not a moral stigma! (Second edition, 227)

Mid. "It relieved me somewhat to learn that in alcoholics the will is amazingly weakened when it comes to combating liquor, though it often remains strong in other respects. My incredible behavior in the face of a desperate desire to stop was explained." Again, Silkworth offers Bill (and by extension the reader) an alternate explanation for his inability to stop or stay stopped. One can almost imagine Silkwoth saying to him, "Bill, you're not crazy or weak-willed. You're alcoholic!"

Bot. "But [self-knowledge was not the answer], for the frightful day came when I drank once more." This theme – that "the actual or potential alcoholic, with hardly an exception, will be *absolutely unable to stop drinking on the basis of self-knowledge*" (39) – is given special attention in Chapter 3. Thus, from Fred's story:

As soon as I regained my ability to think, I went carefully over that [slip] in Washington. *Not only had I been off guard, I had made no fight whatever against the first drink. This time I had not thought of the consequence at all.* I had commenced to drink as carelessly as though the cocktails were ginger ale . . .what I had learned of alcoholism did not occur to me at all. . .I saw that will power and self-knowledge would not help in those strange mental blank spots. (41)

Bot. "After a time I returned to the hospital." Reference to second treatment at Towns; mid-summer, 1934. (*PIO*, 108)

Page 8

Top. "No words can tell of the loneliness and despair I found in that bitter morass of self-pity. . .I had met my match. I had been overwhelmed. Alcohol was my master." Expression of powerlessness and unmanageability also evident in these lines from Chapter 11, "A Vision For You":

> The less people tolerated us, the more we withdrew from society, from life itself. As we became subjects of King Alcohol, shivering denizens of his mad realm, the chilling vapor that is loneliness settled won. It thickened, ever becoming blacker. . . (151)

> Someday he will be unable to image life either with alcohol or without it. Then he will know loneliness such as few do. He will be at the jumping off place. He will wish for the end. (152)

☞ Bill's pride is in ruins. King Alcohol is readying him to embrace a spiritual (vs. medical, psychological, intellectual, etc.) solution to his problem. See also Chapter 4, "We Agnostics": "Faced with alcoholic destruction, we soon became as open minded on spiritual matters as we had tried to be on other questions. In this respect, alcohol was a great persuader." (48, top). This same idea can be found in Chet R's story, "It Might Have Been Worse": "The fact that A.A. is a spiritual program didn't scare me or raise any prejudice in my mind. I couldn't afford the luxury of prejudice. I had tried my way and had failed." (Second ed., 392)

Mid. Armistice Day. Renamed Veteran's Day in 1954, it is celebrated on November 11.

Mid. "I was soon to be catapulted into what I like to call the fourth dimension of existence." Reference to spiritual awakening. See also page 25, first paragraph: "We have found much of heaven and we have been rocketed into a fourth dimension of existence of which we had not even dreamed."

Bot. "Near the end of that bleak November [1934] . . ." The exact date of Ebby's call on Bill is apparently lost to history.

Bot. "The cheery voice of an old school friend. . ." The voice: Edwin "Ebby" Thacher (see Cast of Characters). The school: Burr and Burton Seminary in Manchester, Vermont. Bill attended Burr and Burton from 1909 to 1913. (*PIO*, 33, 35)

Page 9

Bot. ". . .he told how two men had appeared in court, persuading the judge to suspend his commitment. They had told of a simple religious idea and a practical program of action." The two men, both Oxford Groupers, were

Rowland Hazard (see Cast of Characters, and "a certain American business man," 26-28), and Cebra Graves.

☞ Arrested for discharging his shotgun at pigeons that had lighted on the freshly painted roof of the Thacher house in Manchester, Vermont (*PIO*, 114-115), Ebby was released into Rowland's care, schooled in the tenets of the Oxford Group, and lead into his first period of sobriety. (*NG*, 9) Some time later he found lodging at Calvary Rescue Mission (part of Calvary Episcopal Church, Oxford Group headquarters in the United States) at 246 East 23rd Street, New York City. It was while there that, learning of Bill's losing battle with the bottle (*PIO*, 115), Ebby decided to pay a visit to his friend and sometime drinking buddy. (Service or helpfulness to others was one of the major tenets of the Oxford Group. Thus as Rowland – recovering alcoholic – carried a message of hope and salvation to Ebby, so Ebby – now himself a recovering alcoholic – sought to carry the same message to another hopeless drunk.)

☞ Elaborating on the "practical program of action" in an article appearing in the "American Journal of Psychiatry" (Vol. 106, 1949), Bill observed:

> The particular practices [Ebby] had selected for himself were simple:
>
> 1. He admitted he was powerless to solve his own problem.
> 2. He got honest with himself as never before; made an examination of conscience.
> 3. He made a rigorous confession of his personal defects.
> 4. He surveyed his distorted relations with people, visiting them to make restitution.
> 5. He resolved to devote himself to helping others in need, without the usual demand for personal prestige or material gain.
> 6. By meditation he sought God's direction for his life and help to practice these principles at all times.
>
> This sounded pretty naïve to me. Nevertheless my friend stuck to the plain tale of what had happened – no evangelizing. He related how practicing these precepts, his drinking had unaccountably stopped. Fear and isolation left and he had received considerable peace of mind. With no hard disciplines nor any great resolve, these attributes began to appear the moment he conformed. Though sober but months, he felt he had a basic answer. Wisely avoiding any argument, he then took leave. The spark that was to become Alcoholics Anonymous had been struck.

☞ By November or December 1939, the fledgling fellowship of Alcoholics Anonymous had made its final break with the Oxford Group. (*NW, 94*) Several reasons have been cited for this parting (*PTP*, xvi; *PIO*,170-173), among them:

- The wish of many alcoholic members to focus exclusively on helping other alcoholics.
- The young fellowship's desire to distance itself from the growing notoriety of Frank Buchman, Oxford Group founder.
- The Catholic Church discouraged its members from joining other religious bodies, something the Oxford Group was perceived to be.
- The use of tobacco products was disapproved by the Oxford Group.
- The Oxford Group's Four Absolutes and principle of aggressive evangelism – both major tenets – proved counter-productive in working with alcoholics.

Page 10
Mid. "That war-time day in old Winchester Cathedral. . ." Reference to spiritual experience alluded to on page 1.

Page 11
Mid. "But [Ebby] sat before me, and he made the point-blank declaration that God had done for him what he could not do for himself." A statement of step two: "Came to believe that a Power greater than ourselves could restore use to sanity [could lift the alcoholic obsession]." Further expressions of the step two messages of hope may be found on page 25:

> The central fact of our lives today is the absolute certainty that our Creator has entered into our hearts and lives in a way which is indeed miraculous. He has commenced to accomplish those things for us which we could never do by ourselves.

page 60, line (c):

> God could and would [lift our alcoholic obsession] if He were sought.

and page 84, top:

> We will suddenly realize that God is doing for us what we could not do for ourselves.

Should the reader wrestle with or reject the idea of a Supreme Being he might consider amending the above to read: "But [Ebby] sat before me, and he made the point-blank declaration that [reliance on the Oxford Group] had done for him what he could not do for himself" – stay sober!

☞ Plugging Ebby's release from bondage into the text's conversion template (60) we have:

(a) Ebby was alcoholic and could not manage his own life. (*Step One*)

(b) Probably no human power could have relieved his obsession to drink. (*Step One*)

(c) God could and would lift Ebby's obsession if He were sought. (*Step Two*)

- Or -

(a) Ebby was alcoholic and could not manage his own life. (*Step One*)

(b) Ebby could not relieve himself of the obsession to drink. (*Step One*)

(c) The Oxford Group could and would lift Ebby's obsession if he participated in its practices. (*Step Two*)

☞ Despite Bill's critique of organized religion, his grandfather's "good natured contempt of some church folk and their doings," (10) his rebelliousness, intellectual pride, and reflection on the problem of evil (how can one reconcile the idea of a loving, omnipotent God with the overabundance of apparent evil and wrong in the world) – despite all this, Bill cannot deny or doubt the bottom line: He's drunk, Ebby's not!

> That floored me. It began to look as though religious people were right after all. Here was something at work in [Ebby's] heart which had done the impossible. My ideas about miracles were drastically revised right then. Never mind the musty past; here sat a miracle directly across the kitchen table. He shouted great tidings. (11)

Today, of course, such great tidings continue to be shouted across the AA tables throughout the world: "Each day my friend's simple talk in our kitchen multiplies itself in a widening circle of peace on earth and good will to [all]." (16)

Page 12

Mid. "My friend suggested what then seemed a novel idea. He said, '*Why don't you choose your own conception of God?*'" A restatement of Ebby's novel idea is found in Chapter 7, "Working With Others": "If the man be agnostic or atheist, make it emphatic that *he does not have to agree with your conception of God. He can choose any conception he likes, provided it makes sense to him.*" (93)

☞ If the man or woman is an atheist, s/he is not likely to agree with any conception of God. On the other hand, s/he may well be desperate enough to accept the idea of fellowship or group as a higher power.

Mid. "That statement hit me hard. It melted the icy intellectual mountain in whose shadow I had lived and shivered many years. I stood in the sunlight at last." The previously referred to problem of self – here masquerading as intellectual pride – falls away. Bills stands again in the presence of his God (see above, spiritual awakening at Winchester Cathedral, page 1). A defense against King Alcohol is at hand.

Conceptually, we have:

Problem: Powerlessness	Obstacle: Self	Solution: Power
Over Alcohol/Drugs	Intellectual Pride	Higher Power

Mid. *"It was only a matter of being willing to believe in a Power greater than myself. Nothing more was required of me to make my beginning.* I saw that [spiritual] growth could start from that point." Reference to the principle of *willingness,* which, along with *honesty* and *open-mindedness,* are the three essentials – the HOW – of recovery. (Appendix II)

☞ Two additional references to willingness as key to spiritual development are found in Chapter 4, "We Agnostics":

> We found that as soon as we were able to lay aside prejudice and express even a willingness to believe in a Power greater than ourselves, we commenced to get results. . . (46)

> We needed to ask ourselves but one short question. 'Do I now believe, or am I even willing to believe, that there is a Power greater than myself?'. . . It has been repeatedly proven among us that upon this simple cornerstone a wonderfully effective spiritual structure can be built. (47)

Willingness as a necessary condition is also cited on the first page of Chapter 5: "If you have decided you want what we have and are willing to go to any lengths to get it – then you are ready to take certain steps."

Bot. "Thus was I convinced that God is concerned with us humans when we want Him enough." See again reference to spiritual longing at Winchester Cathedral, page 1. Also consider the next paragraph, the mid-paragraph on page 28, and the last line on page 57.

Bot. "But soon the sense of His presence had been blotted out by worldly clamors, mostly those within myself." The problem of self – here Bill's unbridled quest for fame and fortune – as obstacle to Higher Power relationship. In essence, having thanked his God for coming to his aid in Winchester Cathedral, Bill then returned to *his* self-directed agenda: to become the captain of "vast enterprises." (1) (See again Big Book Philosophy, Parts I and II.)

Page 13

Top. "At the hospital I was separated from alcohol for the last time." (Towns Hospital; December 11-18, 1934). The time frame inclusive of Ebby's November visit and Bill's final admission to Towns is truncated here. Surrender does not occur at once. Several days following his initial visit, Ebby again calls on Bill (*PIO,* 116); and in early December an intoxicated Mr. Wilson attends an Oxford Group meeting at Calvary Rescue Mission. (Ibid.). It is only after this tour of Cavalry and two to three more days of drinking (*PIO,* 119) that Bill walks into Towns, beer bottle in hand, for his third and final treatment.

Top. "Treatment seemed wise, for I showed signs of delirium tremens." The most critical form of alcohol withdrawal syndrome. Name highlights its two key components: delirium (hallucinations, confusion, and disorientation), and tremens (heightened autonomic nervous activity, agitation, fast pulse, and fever). Either may dominate. (*LG,* 112).

Top. "There I humbly offered myself to God, as I then understood Him, to do with me as he would. I placed myself unreservedly under His care and direction." For more developed expressions of surrender we have the Third Step Prayer on page 63:

> God, I offer myself to Thee—to build with me and do with me as Thou wilt. Relieve me of the bondage of self, that I may better do Thy will. Take away my difficulties, that victory over them may bear witness to those I would help of Thy Power, Thy Love, and Thy Way of life. May I do Thy will always!

And the Seventh Step Prayer in page 76:

> My Creator, I am now willing that you should have all of me, good and bad. I pray that you now remove from me every single defect of character which stands in the way of my usefulness to you and my fellows. Grant me strength, as I go out from here, to do your bidding. Amen.

Top. "I admitted for the first time that of myself I was nothing; that without Him I was lost." Quite the contrast with this boastful offering from pre-surrender days: "My talent for leadership, I imagined, would place me at the head of vast enterprises which I would manage with the utmost assurance." (1) (See again, Big Book Philosophy, Part III.)

☞ One of the *spiritual truths* revealed to Bill (and by implication the reader) in working step one is that he is *not* God, in control, or self-sufficient.
Top. "I ruthlessly faced my sins. . ." Spiritual kin to step four: "Made a searching and fearless moral inventory of ourselves."

". . . and became willing to have my new-found Friend take them away, root and branch." The spiritual antecedent of steps six and seven, respectively:

"Were entirely ready to have God remove all these defects of character," and, "Humbly asked Him to remove our shortcomings."

☞ See also Ebby's practical program of action, study guide page 57

Mid. "My schoolmate [Ebby] visited me, and I fully acquainted him with my problems and deficiencies." Oxford Group tenet of *confession;* AA step five: "Admitted to God, to ourselves, and to another human being the exact nature of our wrongs."

Mid. "We made a list of people I had hurt or toward whom I felt resentment." AA's step eight: "Made a list of all persons we had harmed, and became willing to make amends to them all."

Mid. "I was to right all such matters to the utmost of my ability." *Restitution;* later AA's ninth spiritual activity: "Made direct amends to such people wherever possible, except when to do so would injure them or others."

Bot. "I was to sit quietly when in doubt, asking only for direction and strength to meet my problems as He would have me." Oxford Group tenet of "relying upon God's guidance and carrying it out in everything we do or say," (*PTP,* Book II, 8); AA's step eleven: "Sought through prayer and meditation to improve our conscious contact with God *as we understood Him,* praying only for knowledge of His will for us and the power to carry that out." The same Oxford teaching is expressed in these two citations from Chapter 6:

> In thinking about our day we may face indecision. We may not be able to determine which course to take. Here we ask God for inspiration, an intuitive thought or a decision. We relax and take it easy. We don't struggle. We are often surprised how the right answers come after we have tried this for a while. (86)

> As we go through the day we pause, when agitated or doubtful, and ask for the right thought or action. We constantly remind ourselves we are no longer running the show, humbly saying to ourselves many times each day 'Thy will be done.' (87-88)

☞ Unlike AA's twelve steps, the Oxford Group's tenets were not numbered or hung on meeting room walls.

Bot. "Never was I to pray for myself, except as my requests bore on my usefulness to others." Admonition against bargaining with one's Higher Power or praying for self-centered ends; that is, entreaties that take the form, "Dear God, help me out of [insert crisis] and I'll never drink again." This cautionary word is repeated in Chapter 6, page 87: "We ask especially for freedom from self-will, and are careful to make no request for ourselves only . . . We are careful never to pray for our own selfish ends. Many of us have wasted a lot of time doing that and it doesn't work."

Page 14

Top. "Simple, but not easy; a price had to be paid. It meant the destruction of self-centeredness." Again, reference to the problem of self – the root of our troubles (62) – as a fundamental block to the grace of a Higher Power.

Top. "I must turn in all things to the Father of Light who presides over us all." A directing of one's will toward God, or working of steps three ("Made a decision to turn our will and our lives over to the care of God *as we understood Him,"*), and eleven ("Sought through prayer and meditation to improve our conscious contact with God *as we understood Him,* praying only for knowledge of his will for us and the power to carry that out"). Thus, from page 85: "Every day is a day when we must carry the vision of God's will into all of our activities"; and page 87: "We usually conclude the period of [morning] meditation with a prayer that we be shown all through the day what our next step is to be, that we be given whatever we need to take care of such problems."

Top. "These were revolutionary and drastic proposals, but the moment I fully accepted them, the effect was electric. . ." Reference to Bill's "hot flash" or spiritual awakening. Vanquished by King Alcohol, despairing of finding release from the merciless obsession,

> the last vestige of pride, the last trace of obstinacy crushed out of him, still he knew he wanted to live.

> His fingers relaxed a little on the footboard, his arms slowly reached out and up. 'I want," he said aloud. "I want. . .'

> 'Oh, God,' he cried, and it was the sound not of a man, but of a trapped and crippled animal. 'If there is a God, show me. Show me. Give me some sign.'

> As he formed the words, in that very instant he was aware first of a light, a great white light that filled the room, then he suddenly seemed caught up in a kind of joy, an ecstasy such as he would never find words to describe. It was as though he were standing high on a mountaintop and a strong clear wind blew against him, around him, through him – but it seemed a wind not of air, but of spirit – and as this happened he had the feeling that he was stepping into another world, a new world of consciousness, and everywhere now there was a wonderful feeling of Presence which all his life he had been seeking. Nowhere had he ever felt so complete, so satisfied, so embraced.
> This happened. And it happened as suddenly and as definitely as one may receive a shock from an electrode, or feel heat when a hand is placed close to a flame. Then when it passed, when the light slowly dimmed, and the ecstasy subsided – and whether this was a matter or much longer he never knew; he was beyond any

reckoning of time – the sense of Presence was still there about him, within him. And with it there was still another sense, a sense of rightness. No matter how wrong things seemed to be, there were as they were meant to be. There could be no doubt of ultimate order in the universe, the cosmos was not dead matter, but a part of the living Presence, just as he was part of it. (*BW, 201*)

Bill Wilson was 39 years old when he had his "white light" experience. He was now ready to be used by his God to help lead a people out of King Alcohol's mad realm.

☞ Referencing the three pertinent ideas on page 60, we have:

(a) Bill was defeated by King Alcohol. (*Step One*)
(b) Bill could not relieve himself of the merciless obsession. (*Step One*)
(c) God could and would lift Bill's obsession if He were sought. (*Step Two*)

☞ The reader is cautioned against reading into Bills transforming experience – sudden and spectacular as it was – a *permanent* lifting of his alcoholic obsession. Bill was not cured. Nor was his walk on the sober side of life without its challenges. King Alcohol would continue to tap him on the shoulder, one time in Akron, Ohio in May 1935. It was this encounter – and Bill's response to it – that was to climax in the founding of Alcoholics Anonymous (see Foreword to Second Edition and Chapter 11, beginning page 153, bottom).

☞ Either Ebby or Rowland furnished Bill with a copy of William James' *Varieties of Religious Experience* following his conversion experience. As Silkworth's explanation of alcoholism as an allergy and obsession provided context to Bill's own struggle with drink, so James' lecture on conversion provided both context and credibility to Bill's "white light" experience. (*PIO,* 125)

☞ Bill's letting go or readiness "to do anything, anything" finds alternate expression in these wondrous words of surrender from Chet R.:

> There comes a time when you don't want to live and are afraid to die. Some crisis brings you to a point of making a decision to do something about your drinking problem. Try anything. Help which you once continually rejected, suggestions once turned aside are finally accepted in desperation. ("It Might Have Been Worse," Second edition, 386-87)

☞ Skeptics have suggested that Bill's awakening was less about the Divine than it was alcohol-induced psychosis; that he (and others) confused delusions and hallucinations incidental to bathtub gin and/or his belladonna treatment with a genuine spiritual illumination. James' lecture on mysticism in *The Varieties* may be instructive here. Referencing a number of sudden conversions or mystical states produced by intoxicants – so-called *anesthetic revelations* – James offers the following observations on beverage alcohol:

> "The sway of alcohol over mankind is unquestionably due to its power to stimulate the mystical faculties of human nature, usually crushed to earth by the cold facts and dry criticism of the sober hour. Sobriety diminishes, discriminates, and says no; drunkenness expands, unites, and says yes. It is in fact the great exciter of the *Yes* function in man. It brings its votary from the chill periphery of things to the radiant core. It makes him for the moment one with truth. Not through mere perversity do men run after it. . .and it is part of the deeper mystery and tragedy of life that whiffs and gleams of something that we immediately recognize as excellent should be vouchsafed to so many of us only in the fleeting earlier phases of what in its totality is so degrading a poisoning. The drunken consciousness is one bit of the mystic consciousness . . ." (*VR*, 387)

Remember too that for James, conversion or change need not be rooted in religion. Nor is its value to be ascertained through an examination of its origin, but by an assessment of what it attains. That deliverance from the bottle – first for Bill, then for hundreds of thousands more – followed his experience in Towns cannot be disputed. Regarded in this light, the specific genesis of Bill's sudden and profound transformation seems a moot point.

Mid. "God comes to most men gradually, but His impact on me was sudden and profound." See Appendix II, "Spiritual Experience."

Bot. "While I lay in the hospital the thought came that there were thousands of hopeless alcoholics who might be glad to have what had been so freely given me [by Ebby]." Part of the spiritual overflow of Bill's conversion experience: the vision of a mutual support program.

☞ "Faith without works was dead. . ." (James 2:14-26) This theme, that faith alone is insufficient to bring about recovery, that faith must be reflected in action, self-sacrifice and works if the alcoholic is to realize deliverance from the bottle, is given considerable play in the text.

Page 15
Top. "My wife and I abandoned ourselves with enthusiasm to the idea of helping other alcoholics to a solution of their problems." Again, faith without works is dead.

Top. "I was not too well at the time, and was plagued by waves of self-pity and resentment. This sometimes nearly drove me back to drink, but I soon found that when all other measures failed, work with another alcoholic would save the day." A suggested antidote to self-centered preoccupation: losing oneself in the work of helping another. From the first paragraph to Chapter 7: "Practical experience shows that nothing will so much insure immunity from drinking as intensive work with other alcoholics. It works when other activities fail." (87)

☞ Again, Bill's hot flash or white light experience did not cure him of his alcoholism nor provide a roadmap around the raindrops.

Bot. "In one western city and its environs. . ." Cleveland, Ohio (*RG, 129)*

Bot. "We meet frequently so that newcomers may find the fellowship they seek." Additional references to meetings (formal and informal) may be found in Chapter 11, "A Vision For You," pages 160-63).

☞ **The slogan, "Don't drink. Go to meetings. And read the Big Book," is *not* found in the Big Book.** The thinking of early AA members was that meeting attendance, while "desirable," was not necessary to maintaining abstinence. Of vital importance, however, were morning devotion and a Higher Power relationship. (*DB*; 131,137) This premium on quiet time and conscious contact is reflected in the treatment of Step Eleven in Chapter 6: "On awakening let us think about the twenty-four hours ahead. We consider our plans for the day. Before we begin, we ask God to direct our thinking. . ." (86) And also in the following paragraph: In thinking about our day we may face indecision. We may not be able to determine which course to take. Here we ask God for inspiration, an intuitive thought or a decision."

Page 16
Top. "An alcoholic in his cups is an unlovely creature." See also page 18, top: "An illness of this sort . . . involves those about us in a way no other human sickness can."; and page 82, bottom: "The alcoholic is like a tornado roaring his way through the lives of others. . ."

☞ Alcoholics obviously have no monopoly on self-will. Nor is an alcoholic's self-willed behavior exclusively a feature of intoxication. Drink certainly exacerbates, but abstinence alone doesn't eliminate.)

Top. "One poor chap committed suicide in my home." Bill C., a Canadian-born attorney, asphyxiated himself in the summer of 1936. (*LR, 105*)

Mid. "Each day my friend's simple talk in our kitchen multiplies itself in a widening circle of peace on earth and good will to men." Reference to Ebby T's visit in late November 1934.

☞ This ministering with the *language of the heart* (*LH,* 243) also shines in Bill initial meeting with Dr. Bob on May 12, 1935. Of this visit, Dr. Bob later observed:

> Of far more importance was the fact that he was the first living human with whom I had ever talked, who knew what he was talking about in regard to alcoholism from actual experience. In other words, he talked my language. (180)

☞ And again from Foreword to Third Edition, final paragraph: "Each day, somewhere in the world, recovery begins when one alcoholic talks with another alcoholic, sharing experience, strength, and hope."

Chapter 2

There Is A Solution

Summary – Shouts the good news: There is help, there is hope, there is a way out of King Alcohol's "mad realm." (151) Brings into sharp focus the alcoholic's powerlessness over the merciless obsession, and her need for a Higher Power relationship as her defense against the first drink. Directs her attention to "the hopelessness and futility of life as [she] had been living it," and spells out the two alternatives commonly faced by the time she reaches AA or the treatment door:

> If you are as seriously alcoholic as we were, we believe there is no middle-of-the-road solution. We were in a position where life was becoming impossible, and if we had passed into the region from which there is no return through human aid, we had but two alternative: One was to go on to the bitter end, blotting out the consciousness of our intolerable situation as best we could; and the other, to accept spiritual help. (25)

Top. "Nearly all have recovered. They have solved the drink problem." *Not* recovered or solved in the sense of cured and fixed, never to be considered again. But in the sense of problem unmasked and arrested. See again Foreword To First Edition for a comment on use of word recover in past tense.

Bot. "The feeling of having shared in a common peril is one element in the powerful cement which binds us . . .We [also] have a way out. . .upon which we can join in brotherly and harmonious action." Thus from "The Keys To The Kingdom":

> I have a wealth of friends and, with my A.A. friends, an unusual quality of fellowship. For, to these people, I am truly related. First, through mutual pain and despair, and later, through mutual objectives and new-found faith and hope. (Second edition, 312)

Bot. "We have a way out on which we can absolutely agree . . .This is the great news this book carries to those who suffer from alcoholism." A step two message of hope (a Power greater than ourselves restored us to sanity), and working of step twelve ("to carry this message to alcoholics"). The idea of a book carrying a message of hope or deliverance is also found on page 19 ("How then shall we present that which has been so freely given us? We have concluded to publish an anonymous volume setting forth the problem as we see it."), and in these lines from Chapter 11, page 153:

> Our hope is that when this chip of a book is launched on the word tide of alcoholism, defeated drinkers will seize upon it, to follow its suggestions. Many, we are sure, will rise to their feet and

march on. They will approach still other sick ones and fellowships of Alcoholics Anonymous may spring up in each city and hamlet, havens for those who must find a way out.

☞ *The Way Out* was one of the favored titles for the Big Book. (*PIO*, 202-03)

Page 18
Top. "An illness of this sort. . .involves those about us in a way no other human sickness can." See also page 82, beginning last paragraph: "The alcoholic is like a tornado roaring his way through the lives of others."

☞ Perhaps surprisingly, the recovery portion of the Big Book, including "The Doctor's Opinion," does *not* refer to alcoholism as a disease, but as an illness, malady or allergy. (The term disease appears but once in the recovery section, on the bottom of page 64: "From [resentment] stem all forms of spiritual disease . . .")

Responding to a question following his address to the National [Catholic] Clergy Conference on Alcoholism in 1961, Bill observed:

We have never called alcoholism a disease because, technically speaking, it is not a disease entity. For example, there is no such thing as heart disease. Instead there are many separate heart ailments, or combinations of them. It is something like that with alcoholism. Therefore we did not wish to get in wrong with the medical profession by pronouncing alcoholism a disease entity. Therefore we always called it an illness, or a malady and a far safer term for us to use. ("Alcoholics Anonymous and the Disease Concept of Alcoholism"; Kurtz, Ernest, PhD)

Mid. "*But the ex-problem drinker who has found this solution . . . can generally win the entire confidence of another alcoholic in a few hours.*" See again Ebby's effort to carry the message to Bill (Chapter 1, page 9 onward). "Dr. Bob's Nightmare" also speaks of the "language of the heart" or the ministering power of twelfth step work:

The question which might naturally come into your mind would be: 'What did [Bill] do or say that was different from what others had done or said?' It must be remembered that I had read a great deal and talked to everyone who knew, or thought they knew anything about the subject of alcoholism . . . *Of far more importance was the fact that he was the first living human with whom I who ever talked, who knew what he was talking about in regard to alcoholism from actual experience. In other words, he talked my language.* He knew all the answers, and certainly not because he had picked them up in his reading. (180)

☞ It should be noted that Dr. Bob's walk in recovery begins *in relationship* with another drunk – not in a book or solitary reflection, or at a workshop on alcoholism. Recovery (spiritual growth) is first and last about living in relationship with self, others, Higher Power and the world about one. Books and workshops certainly have their place. Rarely, however, are they satisfactory substitutes for connections (thus the tendency of addiction counsellors and therapists, especially in residential programs, to admonish: put down of book and take up the talk).

Page 19

Top. "After such an approach many take up their beds and walk again." See, for example, Dr. Bob and Bill's twelfth step call on Bill Dotson ("the man on the bed") on pages 156-158. (Bill D's story, "Alcoholic Anonymous Number Three," is also in the Personal Stories section of editions two, three and four.)

Top. "We feel that elimination of our drinking is but a beginning. A much more important demonstration of our principles lies before us in our respective homes, occupations and affairs." Abstinence as necessary condition of a spiritually-centered life. Lifestyle itself reflected in one's conduct, works, and relations, as per step twelve: "Having had a spiritual awakening as the result of these steps, we tried to carry this message to alcoholics, and to *practice these principles in all our affairs.*" (Italics added.)

Mid. "If we keep on the way we are going. . ." Chiefly by word of mouth or direct work with other alcoholics.

Mid. "We have concluded to publish an anonymous volume setting forth the problem as we see it." The Big Book as a written twelfth step call:

> I stayed up all night reading that book. For me it was a wonderful experienced. It explained so much I had not understood about myself and, best of all, it promised recovery if I would do a few simple things and be willing to have the desire to drink removed. Here was hope. Maybe I could find my way out of this agonizing existence. Perhaps I could find freedom and peace and be able once again to call my soul my own. ("The Keys Of The Kingdom," Second edition, 309)

See again Birth of the Book; also, third edition story, "Lifesaving Words."

Bot. "Of necessity there will have to be discussion of matters medical, psychiatric, social and religious." The Big Book is a synthesis of ideas borrowed from science, medicine and psychology; transcendental and existential mysticism (*NW,* 7); the Bible, Oxford Group, Christian fundamentalism and temperance movements. The reader anticipating a quiet marriage of these influences, or geometric precision in the book's outlining of problem and solution, is in for an awakening (*not* the spiritual variety).

There is a tension – at times a seeming contradiction – between some of these ideas, and even within single themes themselves. (*VS*, 86) For example, just when the reader is about to embrace the idea of alcoholism as treatable illness, she is confronted with the notion of "a self-imposed crisis [she] could not postpone or evade" (53, middle); told that her "liquor was but a symptom" of being blocked off from her Higher Power (64, top); and reminded that, *"After all, our problems were of our own making. Bottles were only a symbol."* (103) Or having succeeded in peeling away his layers of denial and identifying alcohol behind a life unmanageable, he suddenly finds himself being told: "Selfishness – self-centeredness! That, we think, is the root of our troubles." (62) Or having been welcomed and encouraged to *"choose her own conception of God"* (12), she is later confronted with "an ultimately monarchical conception of God. God [as] the all-powerful Director [62] who wants to be totally in charge of our action." (*VS*, 159).

I think it unlikely that these apparent tensions or contradictions admit to a tidy resolution. Perhaps there's too much here of "something old, something new, something borrowed, something blue." (*BFQ*, 782:10) Or perhaps, as I'd argue, these strains and tensions are all beside the point. Perhaps there's sufficient truth in details to keep the whole afloat. To borrow from Whitman, "Do I contradict myself? Very well then I contradict myself, (I am large, I contain multitudes.)" (*BFQ*, 489:21)

☞ "Bill Wilson. . . used the idea of AA as a *synthetic program*. . .This synthesis. . . would mean taking several existing ideas and blending them into something new that would be of service to troubled alcoholics. In shaping AA, the always-practical Wilson was prepared to use building blocks from any source, *the only proviso being that they had to work and be something a troubled alcoholic would accept."* (*NW*, 7. Italics added.) Thus from "Alcoholics Anonymous In Its Third Decade," a presentation given by Wilson to the New York City Medical Society on Alcoholism, April 28, 1958:

> Perhaps the better way to understand AA's methods and results is to have a look at its beginnings, at that time when medicine and religion entered into their benign partnership with us. This partnership is now the foundation of such success as we have since had.

> *Certainly nobody invented Alcoholics Anonymous.* AA is a synthesis of principles and attitudes which came to us from medicine and from religion. We alcoholics have simply streamlined those forces, adapting them to our special use in a society where they can work effectively. Our contribution was but the missing link in a chain of recovery which is now so significant, and of such promise for the future. [Italics added.]

Bot. "Nothing would please us so much as to write a book which would contain no basis for contention or argument." Authors sought to avoid providing the alcoholic with a ready excuse to throw away the book. Text edited to minimize dogmatic, contentious statements (see, for example, discussion of personal pronoun shift and phrase, "God *as we understand Him*," in Chapter 5).

Bot. "Most of us sense that real tolerance of other people's shortcomings and viewpoints and a respect for their opinions are attitudes which make us more useful to others." Thus, for example, from Chapter 6: "Love and tolerance of others is our code" (84, bottom); and from Chapter 7:

> We are careful never to show intolerance or hatred of drinking as an institution. Experience shows that such an attitude is not helpful to anyone. Every new alcoholic looks for this spirit among us and is immensely relieved when he finds we are not witch-burners. A spirit of intolerance might repel alcoholics whose lives could have been saved, had it not been for such stupidity. (103)

Page 20

Top. ". . . we have recovered from a hopeless condition of mind and body." Alcoholism as a two-fold illness: allergy of the body and obsession of the mind.

Bot. "Now these are commonplace observations on drinkers which we hear all the time." Such observations and their variants (e.g., "He's got no backbone." "You'd think she'd stop for her children's sake."), confuse the nature of the alcoholic's problem and present another obstacle to her recovery. Having borrowed or internalized such messages, the alcoholic regards her drinking through moral spectacles, her inability to cease or limit her use of alcohol as shortcoming. Suffering in silence, she tries again and again to wrest control of the uncontrollable, unwittingly setting the stage for yet more failure and more self-loathing. Should she ever find her way to AA, she likely has a difficult time accepting her problem (it's virtually impossible to *embrace* a problem you're ashamed of having), sharing openly, or connecting with others.

☞ Reminder: Part of the rationale for "The Doctor's Opinion" it is to help challenge "these . . . commonplace observations" by offering the alcoholic a medical take on her problem.

Bot. "Moderate drinkers. . . They can take it or leave it alone." The bona fide social drinker.

☞ A social drinker is *not* an alcoholic who can control her drinking. She has a *qualitatively* different experience with beverage alcohol. To her, alcohol is truly something to be taken or left alone. Indeed, a social drinker's attitude toward alcohol is similar to the alcoholic's attitude to, let's say, an orange – truly something to be had or not had. As alcoholics don't think in terms of controlling, hiding and sneaking, or protecting their supply of oranges, so social drinkers don't think in like terms when it comes to beverage alcohol.

This is not to suggest that social drinkers don't get a little tipsy, giddy, warm and relaxed when they drink. Rather, the sense of relaxation, warmth, and lightheadedness is a sign that they've had enough – and so they stop. To an alcoholic, on the other hand, the warmth and lightheadedness she finds in alcohol is not a signal to stop, but a sign that she is going in the right direction: *Inebriation is at hand!* With apologies to Rudyard Kipling: Social drinkers are social drinkers, and alcoholics are alcoholics, and never the drinkers shall meet. ("The Ballad of East and West," *BFM*, 591:9).

☞ Bill Wilson's initial encounter with beverage alcohol is marked by these spiritually-loaded words: ". . . and then, lo, the miracle! I felt that I belonged where I was, belonged to life; I belonged to the universe; I was a part of things at last." (*PIO*, 56) This is not the response of a social drinker to her first drink, any more than it is the reaction of an alcoholic to his first orange. (Such experiences are, I suspect, the reason why many alcoholics regard their initial encounter with bottled spirits as the onset of their alcoholism. "Miracles" do leave their mark.)

Bot. "Then we have a certain type of hard drinker." Unmanageability without symptoms common to alcohol use disorder, i.e., tolerance (either increased or decreased), craving, withdrawal, loss of control, and continued use despite knowledge of psychological or physical problems related to drinking. (*DSM*, 233-34)

Top. "But what about the real alcoholic? He may start off as a moderate drinker; he may or may not become a continuous hard drinker. . ." One doesn't have to be a daily drinker to meet diagnostic criteria for alcoholism, or to qualify for membership in AA. Alcoholism is not a matter of how much or how often; rather, of inability to moderate or stop in the face of increasing dysfunction and unmanageability.

". . . but at some stage of his drinking career he begins to lose all control of his liquor consumption, once he starts to drink." *Loss of control* or allergy of the body: the alcoholic cannot predict with any degree of certainty when he will stop using once he begins. See also Chapter 4, first paragraph: ". . . or if when drinking, you have little control over the amount you take."

Mid. "He is a real Dr. Jekyll and Mr. Hyde." Reference to *The Strange Case of Dr. Jekyll and Mr. Hyde,* by Scottish author, Robert Louis Stevenson (1850-1894). The kindly Dr. Jekyll discovers a drug by which he can change himself into the sinister Mr. Hyde. (*CEO*) The analogy to beverage alcohol seems obvious. Alcohol-induced transitions are noted in the following:

"The Housewife Who Drank At Home":

> I became one of the most active women in the community. . . But I wasn't happy. I became a Jekyll-and-Hyde person. As long as I worked, as long as I got out, I didn't drink. But I had to get back to that first drink somehow. And when I took that first drink, I was

off on the usual merry-go-round. And it was my home that suffered. My husband, my children saw the other side of me. (Second edition, 379)

"*Me* An Alcoholic?":

When I try to reconstruct what my life was like "before," I see a coin with two faces.

One, the side I turned to myself and the world, was respectable – even, in some ways, distinguished. . . I was listed in "Who's Who in America" as an American who, by distinguished achievement, had arrived. I was, so far as anybody could tell, quite a lad.

The other side of the coin was sinister, baffling. I was inwardly unhappy most of the time. There would be times when the life of respectability and achievement seemed insufferably dull – I had to break out. This I would do by going completely "bohemian" for a night, getting drunk and rolling home with the dawn. (Second edition, 419)

And from Hank Parkhurst's story, "The Unbeliever":

My Lord, the tragedy that sprang out of her eyes when I came home with a breath on me . . . and fear. The smiles wiped off the kids' faces. Terror stalking through the house. Yes . . . that changed it from a home into a house. Not drunk yet, but they knew what was coming. My Hyde was moving in. (First edition, 198)

Page 22

Top. ". . . he may have liquor concealed all over his house to be certain no one gets his entire supply away from him. . ." Protecting supply. A list of Dr. Bob's favored hiding places is found in his story, "Dr. Bob's Nightmare." (Second edition, 176-77.

Top. "As matters grow worse, he begins to use a combination of high-powered sedative and liquor to quiet his nerves so he can go to work." Reference to *cross-addiction:* substitution of one type of drug (a high-powered sedative) for another (alcohol) in the same class of drugs (in this instance soporifics or central nervous system depressants). It is this phenomenon that allows the alcoholic to be withdrawn from ethyl alcohol by use of another depressant, Librium. It also allowed for AA's co-founder, Dr. Bob, to substitute "goof balls" (barbiturates) for alcohol to help quiet the morning jitters so that he could go to work to earn enough money to buy more liquor to put himself to sleep to arise and substitute barbiturates for alcohol to quiet the agitation from the previous evening's sedation so that he could go to work to earn enough money to buy more liquor, and so on ad nauseam. (See "Dr. Bob's Nightmare," Second edition, 176-77.)

☞ There is no inherent conflict in being an alcoholic *and* drug addicted member of Alcoholics Anonymous – provided the "desire to stop drinking." (Tradition Three) As Bill observed in his February 1958 *Grapevine* article, "Problems Other Than Alcohol":

> One of the best AAs I know is a man who had been seven years on the needle before he joined up with us. But prior to that, he had been a terrific alcoholic and his history proved it. Therefore he could qualify for AA and this he certainly did.

Bot. "We know that while the alcoholic keeps away from drink, as he may do for months or years, he reacts much like other men." In the absence of drink, there are no well-defined behaviors or characteristics that set apart alcoholic men and women from the population as a whole.

Page 23

Top. "These observations would be academic and pointless if our friend never took the first drink, thereby setting the terrible cycle in motion. Therefore, the main problem of the alcoholic centers in his mind, rather than in his body." The inability of the alcoholic to stop once she starts is of little importance – *provided* she stays away from the first drink . (Consider: What happens to someone allergic to raspberries "would be academic and pointless if our friend never took the first" raspberry). Her problem, therefore, centers not on the allergy of the body (the phenomenon of craving that ensues once she drinks) but on the obsession of the mind (which ensures that she will drink). From this point forward, the Big Book's focus is on the alcoholic's mind or "mental states that precede a relapse" (35), the need for a spiritual solution, and the development of a Higher Power relationship.

☞ It is to help defend her against the obsession of the mind, *not* the allergy of the body, that a Higher Power relationship is recommended. The restoration to sanity cited in Step Two ("Came to believe that a Power greater than ourselves could restore us to sanity") is the *lifting* of the merciless obsession; that is, the obsession with intoxication or controlled drinking.

Bot. "There is the obsession that somehow, someday, they will beat the game." *Obsession* as preoccupation with control, with trying to prove that "we could drink like other people" (30). Additional text references to obsession with control *or* inebriation include:

- "After they have succumbed to the desire again [obsession] . . . and the phenomenon of craving develops [allergy], they pass through the well-known stages of a spree, emerging remorseful, with a firm resolution not to drink again." ("The Doctor's Opinion," xxvii)

- "A tumbler full of gin followed by half a dozen bottles of beer would be required if I were to eat any breakfast. Nevertheless, I still thought I could control the situation, and there were periods of sobriety which renewed my wife's hope." (5)

- "Liquor ceased to be a luxury; it became a necessity." (5)

- "The almost certain consequences that follow taking even a glass of beer do not crowd into the mind to deter us. If these thoughts occur, they are hazy and readily supplanted with the old threadbare idea that this time we shall handle ourselves like other people." (24)

- "The alcoholic may say to himself in the most casual way, 'It won't burn me this time, so here's how.'" (24)

- "The idea that somehow, someday he will control and enjoy his drinking is the great obsession of every abnormal drinker. The persistence of this illusion is astonishing. Many pursue it into the gates of insanity or death." (30)

- "'*Two:* Your husband is showing lack of control, for he is unable to stay on the water wagon even when he wants to. . .He admits this is true, but is positive that he will do better. . .He is remorseful after serious drinking bouts and tells you he wants to stop. But when he gets over the spree, he begins to think once more how he can drink moderately next time." (109)

- "He admits he cannot drink like other people, but does not see why. He clings to the notion that he will yet find a way to do so." (110)

- "Never could we recapture the great moments of the past. There was an insistent yearning to enjoy life as we once did and a heartbreaking obsession that some new miracle of control would enable us to do it." (151)

- "They didn't have to tell me that alcoholism was a sickness. When you take a bottle and lock the door and go in by yourself, that is death." ("The Independent Blonde," Second edition, 535)

- "I could not see why I couldn't drink like a gentleman, and that was my primary ambition – until I landed in A.A. This pattern deepened and became worse. I became a constant drinker with a terrific fight to control the amount of my consumption each day." (Abby G., "He Thought He Could Drink Like A Gentleman," Second edition, 214)

- "The successful demonstration I had made of my problems in other respects convinced me that someday I was going to be able to drink like a gentleman." ("He Thought He Could Drink Like A Gentleman," Second edition, 214)

• "When I was about forty-seven, after indulging in all kinds of self-deception to control my drinking, I arrived at a period when I felt convinced I had to have so much alcohol every day and that the real problem was to control how much." ("He Thought He Could Drink Like A Gentleman," Second edition, 214)

• "My drinking habits increased in spite of my struggle for control." ("The Keys Of The Kingdom," Second edition, 305)

• "Never having enough, always craving more, the obsession for alcohol gradually dominated all my activities, particularly while traveling. Drink planning became more important than any other plans." ("It Might Have Been Worse," Second edition, 384)

☞ Throughout the text, obsession as the dogged pursuit of control over alcohol appears to overshadow obsession as craving or preoccupation with intoxication. I'm not sure that the urge to drink or get drunk receives fair billing here. My impression is that the experience of intoxication has a greater or more immediate hold over the alcoholic than does the yearning for control, and that the so-called obsession to "prove we could drink like other men" (30) is less true obsession than reaction to the threat of denied inebriation, a determined and persistent refusal to accept that, to paraphrase a cliché, the alcoholic can't have her alcohol and drink it too (more about this in the study of Chapter 3).

Page 24
Top. "At a certain point in the drinking of every alcoholic, he passes into a state where the most powerful desire to stop drinking is of absolutely no avail. This tragic situation *has already arrived in practically every case long before it is suspected.*" (Italics added.) The insidious nature of alcoholism (and the addictive process in general): the potential alcoholic is within its grip long before its grip is revealed to the newborn alcoholic. From "Women Suffer Too": "With a creeping insidiousness, drink had become more important than anything else. It no longer gave me pleasure – it merely dulled the pain – but I *had* to have it. I was bitterly unhappy." (Second edition, 226)

☞ The person who berates or belittles himself for falling victim to King Alcohol, for not putting down the bottle before he lost control, or failing to spot powerlessness on the horizon, might wish to reassess her thinking in light of this insidious feature. He might also consider why he's so special that *he* should have spotted what legions of others have failed to see. Talk about false pride. (Alternatively, the alcoholic might want to ponder the possible gain of clinging to his self-condemning dialogue. It certainly brings him no closer to a solution for his drinking problem. If anything, it would seem to bind him all the more to it.)

Top. *"The fact is that most alcoholics, for reasons yet obscure, have lost the power of choice in drink. . . We are without defense against the first drink."* The obsession of the mind. See also last paragraph Chapter 3: "Once more: The alcoholic at certain times has no effective mental defense against the first drink. . .His defense must come from a Higher Power."

Mid. "The almost certain consequences that follow taking even a glass of beer do not crowd into the mind to deter us. If these thoughts occur, they are hazy and readily supplanted with the old threadbare idea that this time we shall handle ourselves like other people." Simple denial: this time will be different; this time I will be able to manage or control my drinking. See also Chapter 3, first paragraph: "The idea that somehow, someday he will control and enjoy his drinking is the great obsession of every abnormal drinker"; and Chapter 11, 151: "There was an insistent yearning to enjoy life as we once did and a heartbreaking obsession that some new miracle of control would enable us to do it."

☞ On the other hand, the alcoholic may know all too well that this time won't be any different than a hundred times before, may know all too well the likely consequence of taking that first drink, may know all this – and yet put up no struggle or resistance, no fight whatsoever. Intoxication is to be had. Unmanageability be damned. This is powerlessness. This is illness run riot!

Mid. "There is a complete failure of the kind of defense that keeps one from putting his hand on a hot stove." Contrast with last paragraph, page 84 (attitude toward alcohol following spiritual awakening or appeal to a Higher Power): "...sanity [the lifting of the alcoholic obsession] will have returned. We will seldom be interested in liquor. If tempted, we [now] recoil from it as from a hot flame." The crux of step two: a Higher Power relationship has accomplished that which self-will or self-knowledge could not.

Bot. "Or perhaps he doesn't think at all. . ." Thus from "Bill's Story," page 5, bottom:

> This [drinking] had to be stopped. I saw I could not take so much as one drink. I was through forever. . .
>
> Shortly afterward I came home drunk. There had been no fight. Where had been my high resolve? I simply didn't know. It hadn't even come to mind. Someone had pushed a drink my way, and I had taken it. Was I crazy? I began to wonder, for such an appalling lack of perspective seemed near being just that.

See also Fred's story, pages 39-42; especially bottom of 41 to top of 4

Bot. "When this sort of thinking [obsession of the mind] is fully established in an individual with alcoholic tendencies, he has probably placed himself beyond human aid. . ." The book is suggesting that short of a spiritual solution – a Higher Power relationship – little can done to save the alcoholic from the grip of King Alcohol. Fortunately for the atheist or agnostic, Higher Power can be spelled in small case letters; that is, a sustained and humble appeal to the AA group itself seems sufficient to bring about this release. (Whether, as may be suggested, this is but the hand of God, Creator or Universal Spirit working though the group, I am content to leave for others to consider.)

Page 25

Top. *"There is a solution."* Trumpets the good news: A Power greater than ourselves has delivered *us* from another power greater than ourselves – the alcohol obsession.

Top. "Almost none of us liked the self-searching, the leveling of our pride, the confession of shortcomings which the process requires for its successful consummation. But we saw that it really worked in others, and we had come to believe in the hopelessness and futility of life as we had been living it." It is not just the bottle that has a hand in alcoholic's undoing, but his centered-on-self – vs. centered-on-God – existence; not just his alcohol-soaked days that bring about ruin, but a spirituality in which he reigns as his own higher power. The alcoholic who attempts to fault King Alcohol for all his woes, who believes that recovery is but a matter of putting the cork in the jug, is missing the boat. More than his drinking must be arrested; his own life philosophy must be confronted and overhauled. (The rationale and mechanism for personal inventory and change is covered more extensively in Chapters 5 and 6 of the text.)

Top. "When, therefore, we were approached. . ." Consider Bill W. being approached by Ebby T. that bleak November afternoon in 1934 (Chapter 1).

". . . by those in whom the problem had been solved. . . " *Problem* denoting obsession of the mind: ". . .the main problem of the alcoholic centers in his mind, rather than in his body" (23, top); and *solved* referring to obsession being lifted or removed: "We have not even sworn off. Instead, the problem has been removed. It does not exist for us." (85, top)

". . .there was nothing left for us but to pick up. . ." Pick up as reference to working step three: "Made a decision to turn our alcohol problem over to the care of God *as we understood him."* See also top of page 59: "Half measures availed us nothing. We stood at the turning point. We asked His protection and care with complete abandon."

". . . kit of spiritual tools laid at our feet." Spiritual tools as inclusive of the twelve steps. (It might also be argued that the Bible and other spiritual or religious literature were included in this kit.)

Mid. ". . . and we have been rocketed into a fourth dimension of existence. . ." Bill's reference to a spiritual experience or awakening (see page 8, middle).

Bot. "He has commenced to accomplish those things for us which we could never do by ourselves." Step two message of hope: "Came to believe that a Power greater than ourselves could restore us to sanity." Reiterated in line (c) of the "three pertinent ideas" on page 62: "That God could and would if He were sought"; and the Twelfth Promise on page 84, top: "We will suddenly realize that God is doing for us what we could not do for ourselves."

☞ The reader more at home with the idea of group as Higher Power is invited to consider this interpretation: "The central fact of our lives today is the absolute certainty that [the program and fellowship of AA] has entered into our hearts and lives in a way which is indeed miraculous. [Connection with AA] has commenced to accomplish those things for us which we could never do by ourselves."

☞ ". . . there is no middle-of-the-road solution." Again, from page 59: "Half measures availed us nothing. We stood at the turning point." Same idea expressed in these lines from Pat M.'s story, "Desperation Drinking":

> And I jumped in with both feet. Someone told me, "When you drank, you didn't get half drunk. You went all the way. In this program there aren't any half way measures. In here you must go all the way too." So I jumped in with both feet. (Second edition, 513)

Bot. ". . . we had but two alternatives. . ." The alcoholic at a turning point: maintain the status quo (her alcohol-centered and sodden existence) or accept spiritual help.

Page 26

Top. "A certain American business man. . ." Rowland Hazard (1881-1945). A biographical sketch of Rowland may be found in the May 1995 issue of the *AA Grapevine.*

Mid. "Above all, he believed he had acquired such a profound knowledge of the inner workings of his mind and its springs that relapse was unthinkable. Nevertheless, he was drunk in a short time." One of the recurrent Big Book themes: self-knowledge (including knowledge of her illness) does *not* provide the alcoholic with an adequate defense against the first drink (the merciless obsession). See again Bill's own painful discovery of this truth on page 7: "Understanding myself now, I fared forth in high hope . . . Surely this was the answer – self-knowledge. But it was not, for the frightful day came when I drank once more." This theme will be revisited in Chapter 3, "More About Alcoholism."

Top. ". . . once in a while, alcoholics have what are called vital spiritual experiences." See discussion of psychic change or spiritual awakening in "The Doctor's Opinion."

Mid. "Ideas, emotions, and attitudes which were once the guiding forces of the lives of these men are suddenly cast to one side, and a completely new set of conceptions and motives begins to dominate them." Illustrative of these changed spiritual scripts are:

"I *can't* stay sober." → "I *can* stay sober!"

"I can *not* drink." → "I *can* not drink!"

"I feel hopeless." → "I feel hopeful!"

☞ A cautionary word: For the *majority* of alcoholics, such transformations occur gradually – *not* suddenly. Too, they do not occur in a vacuum (are not the sole products of self-will or self-knowledge), but within the context of one's *relationships* with others, community and Higher Power. Thus from Appendix II, "Spiritual Experience":

> He finally realizes that he has undergone a profound alteration in his reaction to life [and the bottle]; that such a change could hardly have been brought about by himself alone. What often takes place in a few months could seldom be accomplished by years of self-discipline. With few exceptions our members find that they have tapped an unsuspected inner resource which they presently identify with their own conception of a Power greater than themselves.

For example, the above cited spiritual shift – from "I *can't* stay sober" to "I *can* stay sober" – occurs within *context* of the alcoholic's relationships with program, fellowship and Higher Power.

Additional references to spiritual conversion include:

> A complete change takes place in our approach to life. Where we used to run from responsibility, we find ourselves accepting it with gratitude that we can successfully shoulder it. Instead of wanting got escape some perplexing problem, we experience a thrill of challenge in the opportunity it affords for another application of A.A. techniques, and we find ourselves tackling it with surprising vigor. ("The Keys To The Kingdom," Second edition, 311-312)

And from "He Sold Himself Short":

> This latest part of my life has had a purpose, not in great things accomplished but in daily living. Courage to face each day has replaced the fears and uncertainties of earlier years. Acceptance of things as they are has replaced the old impatient champing at the bit to conquer the world. I have stopped tilting at windmills, and instead have tried to accomplish the little daily tasks, unimportant in themselves, but tasks that are an integral part of living fully. (Second edition, 295).

Bot. ". . . but I have never been successful with an alcoholic of your description." Jung admits to the limitations of his art; acknowledges that science and Western medicine stand powerless before the alcoholic obsession. In its stead, he prescribes a spiritual remedy: a religious conversion experience, which Rowland later finds through his involvement with the Oxford Group. (See Four Founding Moments of AA.)

Bot. "This hope, however, was destroyed by the doctors telling him that while religious convictions were very good, in his case they did not spell the necessary vital spiritual experience."

> Ordinary religious faith isn't enough. What I'm talking about is a transforming experience, a conversion experienced, if you like. I can only recommend that you placed yourself in the religious atmosphere of your own choice, that you recognize your personal hopelessness, and that you cast yourself upon whatever God you think there is. The lightening of the transforming experience may then strike you. This you must try – it is your only way out. ("Alcoholics Anonymous In Its Third Decade"; Presented by Bill Wilson to the New York City Medical Society on Alcoholism, April 28, 1958.)

Page 28

Top. ". . . when he had the extraordinary experience. . .which made him a free man." Reference to Rowland's spiritual or conversion experience in the early 1930s.

Mid. "We have no desire to convince anyone that there is only one way by which faith can be acquired." Again, Big Book written in the spirit of accommodation.

Mid. ". . . are the children of a living Creator with whom we may form a relationship. . ." It is through *relationship* with the Higher Power of her understanding that the alcoholic experiences a lifting of the merciless obsession. Thus from Chapter 3: "The alcoholic at certain times has no effective mental defense against the first drink . . . His defense must come from a Higher Power [relationship]" (43); and from Chapter 7: "Remind the prospect that his recovery is not dependent upon people. It is dependent upon his relationship with God." (99-100)

Page 29

Top. ". . . clear-cut directions are given. . ." The twelve steps. Perhaps the easiest way to think of steps is as a series of directions out of King Alcohol's mad realm to a spiritual awakening or "personality change sufficient to bring about recovery from alcoholism. (Appendix II, Spiritual Experience)

Chapter 3

More About Alcoholism

Summary – Draws upon case histories of relapse to launch a final assault against the alcoholic's denial of his or her problem (step one) and resistance to spiritual help (step two). (*BBD,* Tape 2, Side 1) It reminds the alcoholic that once powerless over alcohol, always powerless over alcohol; illustrates the folly of trying to stop drinking on the basis of self-will or self-knowledge; and, in the final paragraph, again calls the reader's attention to the need for a Higher Power relationship as his or her defense against the merciless obsession: "Once more: The alcoholic at certain times has no effective mental defense against the first drink. Except in a few rare cases, neither he nor any other being can provide such a defense. His defense must come from a Higher Power."

Page 30
Top. "No person likes to think he is bodily and mentally different from his fellows. Therefore, it is not surprising that our drinking careers have been characterized by countless vain attempts to prove we could drink like other people." The chapter appears to finger the quest for "sameness" as underlying the countless vain attempts at controlled drinking. I'm not entirely sure of this. While the desire to prove he can drink like others may play a role in the alcoholic's efforts at controlled use, my sense is that something other than an attempt at physical and mental integrity is at work here.

The experience of intoxication has a singular hold on the alcoholic. It is his salvation and his solution; it is his reason to be. All else pales in comparison; everything else is measured against it. Any threat, real or fancied, to this experience must be answered with equal vigor. Rebukes by family and friends, the closed tavern or liquor store, a loved one's efforts to wrest control of the bottle – the list is countless – each threaten the alcoholic's existence as practicing alcoholic.

None, however, are match to his *own truth* about her drinking. On some level the alcoholic knows that there is something wrong here; *knows that he is alcoholic and that she must stop drinking!* But such a truth is unacceptable. He cannot drink with it. And so the alcoholic buries his truth and drinks on in denial. He tries to masquerade as others. He tries in vain to prove he can do what he knows he cannot: control his liquor.

Ultimately, for the alcoholic to establish long-term residence around the AA tables he must accept more than his powerlessness. He must accept that drinking is no longer an option for him. He must go beyond embracing abstinence. He must renounce intoxication – renounce a turning to objects or events for answers and solutions – as a way of life.

☞ Renouncing a life centered on intoxication entails more than throwing away the bottle. That is the *easy* part. The more challenging work of recovery involves a casting aside of "ideas, emotions and attitudes which were once the guiding forces of the lives of these men [and women]. (27) For example, the desire to fix or flee one's loneliness and pain; the belief that the world – God, parents, society – *owe me*; the search for something for nothing or change on demand. It is to accept that, to borrow the opening line of Scott Peck's *Road Less Travelled,* "life is difficult"; that our problems can't be solved except by solving them (Ibid, 32); and that authorship for our own stories falls squarely in our own laps. While for most this conversion comes slowly, perhaps begrudgingly, it seems both necessary condition for a rich recovery and, ironically, a parting gift from King Alcohol himself.

☞ While the primary focus of this book is understandably on beverage alcohol, the concept of cross-addiction and the large number of *alcohol and drug addicted* members of AA suggest the inclusion of the following little anonymous prayer. I think it speaks well to both the power of addiction, and many an alcoholic or addict's fight and flight against adulthood:

God,
please let there be
one non-addictive
mood-altering drug that
I can use with impunity.
Amen.

Top. "The idea that somehow, someday he will control and enjoy his drinking is the great obsession of every abnormal drinker" (abnormal here being defined as alcoholic). As already noted, my impression is that obsession with the experience of intoxication has a more immediate hold over the alcoholic than does obsession with control; that obsession with control is more automatic response to the threat of denied intoxication than end in itself. After all, control is a non-issue for those who have no stake in drinking or inebriation.

Top. "The persistence of this illusion. . ." Actually less an illusion than simple denial: a psychological defense the alcoholic sets up to protect herself from the fact that alcohol is indeed a problem. Such a defense is automatic and unconscious. (*PD,* 11-12)

Mid. "We learned that we had to *fully concede* to our innermost selves that we were alcoholics. This is the first step in recovery." (Italics added.) While a distinction is sometimes made between admitting and accepting (i.e., "I admit that I'm an alcoholic, though I've yet to fully accept it"), within the context of step one, to admit is to accept is to embrace is to "concede to one's innermost self" one's powerlessness over alcohol. After all, it's unlikely that Bill had the following in mind when considering the first step taken: We admitted we were powerless over alcohol, though not all of us accepted this—that our lives had become unmanageable, though not all of us accepted this, either.

Mid. "We alcoholics are men and women who have lost the ability to control our drinking." Powerless does not mean that every time the alcoholic drinks she will get drunk; or that willpower will never defend her against the first drink. Rather, that she cannot predict with any degree of success how she will fare against the first drink, nor consistently rely upon her own resources to safeguard her from it.

Mid. "We know that no real alcoholic *ever* recovers control." Alcoholism as a chronic illness.

Page 31

Top. "Science may one day accomplish this, but it hasn't done so yet." It seems unlikely that a real alcoholic would actually want to become a social drinker, especially after realizing how little bang for the drink there was in it. Remember, alcoholics have a *qualitatively different reaction* to beverage alcohol than do social drinkers. It's one thing to want to drink soberly and sanely, quite another to want to drink alcoholically *without* the consequences. If science can find a way to do that – have your alcoholism and drink it too – well . . . But hey, isn't this the very sort of "cake and eat it too thinking" that lies at the core of addiction?

Top. "By every form of self-deception and experimentation, they will try to prove themselves exceptions to the rule, therefore nonalcoholic." The rule: "that no real alcoholic *ever* recovers control." (30)

Mid. "Here are some of the methods we have tried [to drink like others]." An attempt to control is an attempt to demonstrate that one is not powerless over alcohol, that one has say over how much and/or how often one drinks, that one is not subject to the rule of allergy and obsession. An attempt to control is an attempt to demonstrate that one *can* drink. (Again, a social drinker does not think in terms of control when having a drink any more than does an alcoholic think in terms of control when having a glass of orange juice.)

Bot. ". . . but you can quickly diagnose yourself. . .try some controlled drinking. Try to drink and stop abruptly." Self-diagnostic test focusing on allergy of the body: attempting to stop after taking the first drink. A second diagnostic tool, this one centering on the obsession of the mind (or attempting to stay away from the first drink) is to be found on top of page 34.

☞ Of course, failed results may simply trigger "the old threadbare idea that [next] time we shall handle ourselves like other people" (24). Which is, after all, a reasonable response for a practicing alcoholic.

Page 32

Top. ". . . we believe that early in our drinking careers most of us could have stopped drinking." See also page 34, top: "As we look back, we feel we had gone on drinking many years beyond the point where we could quit on our will power."

Page 33

Top. "Once an alcoholic, always an alcoholic . . . If we are planning to stop drinking, there must be no reservation of any kind, nor any lurking notion that someday we will be immune to alcohol." See again page 30: "We alcoholics are men and women who have lost the ability to control our drinking. We know that no real alcoholic *ever* recovers control."

Mid. "We doubt if many of them can do it, because none will really want to stop, and hardly one of them, because of the peculiar mental twist [obsession] already acquired, will find he can win out." The insidious nature of alcoholism (and the addictive process in general): the alcoholic is in its grip before its grip is revealed to the alcoholic. Thus, from page 24, top:

> "At a certain point in the drinking of every alcoholic, he passes into a state where the most powerful desire to stop drinking is of absolutely no avail. This tragic situation has already arrived in practically every case long before it is suspected."

Bot. "Potential female alcoholics often turn into the real thing and are gone beyond recall in a few years." From the Butler Center for Research at Hazelden:

> Women are often more susceptible to alcohol-related medical disorders than are men. For example, alcoholic women develop cirrhosis, cardio-myopathy, and brain impairment at the same rate, or sooner than, their male counterparts despite lower lifetime levels of alcohol consumption.

> This accelerated development of physical problems is consistent with other research that shows that, overall, the course of the disease of alcoholism seems to develop somewhat more rapidly among women than men, though the progression of symptoms is quite similar. This phenomenon is known as a 'telescoping effect,' where the time from first heavy drinking to first treatment, or other indicator of major problems, is shortened.

> Why do women have unique health risks associated with heavy alcohol use? Women may have reduced levels of the gastric enzyme [alcohol dehydrogenase] that metabolizes alcohol, resulting in proportionately higher blood alcohol concentrations. In addition, alcohol may increase estrogen-related hormones, such as estradiol. Complicating matters, these two systems may be inter-related, creating synergistic effects. ("Women and Substance Abuse"; *Hazelden Research Update;* January 1999)

Page 34

Top. "If anyone questions whether he has entered this dangerous area, let him try leaving liquor alone for one year. . ." Self-diagnosis focusing on obsession of the mind: attempting to stay away from the first drink.

Mid. "We are assuming, of course, that the reader desires to stop." First half of *step zero* as necessary condition for recovery. From page 58: *"If you have decided you want what we have* and are willing to go to any length to get it — then you are ready to take certain steps." (Italics added.)

Mid. "Whether such a person can quit upon a nonspiritual basis. . ." That is, whether such a person can quit on the basis of self-will or self-knowledge, or without the helping hand of a Power greater than himself, "depends upon the extent to which he has already lost the power to choose whether he will drink or not."

Bot. "This is the baffling feature of alcoholism as we know it. . ." From page 58, bottom: "Remember that we deal with alcohol — cunning, baffling, powerful. Without help it is too much for us."

Page 35

Top. "So we shall describe some of the mental states that precede a relapse into drinking, for obviously this is the crux of the problem." The inability of the alcoholic to stop drinking once she starts is of little practical import — provided, of course, that she doesn't start. The obsession — the mental state that precedes the first drink — is, therefore, the "crux" of the matter. Again from Chapter 2:

> These observations would be academic and pointless if our friend never took the first drink, thereby setting the terrible cycle in motion. Therefore, the main problem of the alcoholic centers in his mind, rather than in his body.

Mid. "Our first example is a friend we shall call Jim." The inclusion of Jim and Fred's woeful tales have a twofold purpose: first, to provide the reader with an additional diagnostic tool — "some of the mental states that precede a relapse into drinking"; and second, "to smash home upon our alcoholic reader as it has been revealed to us out of bitter experience . . . [that] the actual or potential alcoholic, with hardly an exception, will be *absolutely unable to stop drinking on the basis of self-knowledge*" (39).

☞ Self-knowledge as inadequate defense against the first drink was initially seen in Bill's own efforts to stymie the merciless obsession: "Surely this was the answer — self-knowledge. But it was not, for the frightful day came when I drank once more." (7); and later in Rowland H's tussle with King Alcohol: "Above all, he believed he had acquired such a profound knowledge of the inner workings of his mind and its hidden springs that relapse was unthinkable. Nevertheless, he was drunk in a short time." (26) The repeated airing of this theme in Chapter 3 is intended to eliminate any lingering resistance on the reader's part to accept a spiritual prescription as antidote to her alcohol problem; that is, to help ready the alcoholic to embrace a Higher Power relationship as her defense against the first drink.

Bot. "All went well for a time, but he failed to enlarge his spiritual life." Jim's back remained turned to a Power greater than himself. Escape from the bottle, he reckoned, would be had through self-sufficiency.

Bot. "He agreed he was a real alcoholic and in a serious condition." It's a bit unclear as to what Jim was acknowledging in agreeing that he was a real alcoholic. Lines following certainly suggest an awareness of the need for abstinence. Short of this, however, his basic difficulty would seem to be the absence of step one acceptance. That is, Jim cannot at the same time accept that he is without defense against the first drink *and* also believe that self-knowledge will provide him with a sufficient defense against the first drink. If he accepts that he's powerless, then by implication he accepts that he can't keep himself sober; if he believes that he can keep himself sober, that self-knowledge or self-will can shield him from King Alcohol, then he isn't accepting he's powerless. Something has got to give: either denial or the "illusion" of control yields to acceptance; or acceptance devolves into denial. (Fred would appear to share the same basic problem.)

☞ Jim's apparent denial around step one would also seem to explain his failure "to enlarge his spiritual life." An alcoholic is not going to grab the helping hand of AA (step three), even if she believes that AA offers a safe haven for alcoholics (step two), unless she first accepts her devastating powerless over alcohol itself (step one).

Bot. *"He had much knowledge about himself as an alcoholic. Yet all reasons for not drinking were easily pushed aside in favor of the foolish idea that he could take whiskey if only he mixed it with milk!"* Another attempt to control. See again page 31: "By every form of self-deception and experimentation, they will try to prove themselves exceptions to the rule, therefore nonalcoholic."

Page 37
Top. ". . . we call this plain insanity." The insanity of the first drink: this time will be different; this time control will be had!

Mid. "Our sound reasoning failed to hold us in check. The insane idea won out." Powerlessness! The "complete failure of the kind of defense that keeps one from putting his hand on a hot stove." (24)

Bot. "Our behavior is as absurd and incomprehensible with respect to the first drink as that of an individual with a passion, say, for jay-walking." The use of the absurd to help spotlight the absurd.

☞ Note parallels in the jaywalker and typical alcoholic's stories in terms of the evolution of their respective obsessions: from not wanting to stop jaywalking or drinking because it's too much fun, to not being able to stop due to the "peculiar mental twist" acquired.

Page 38

Bot. ". . . we have not gone to the extremes you fellows did, nor are we likely to, for we understand ourselves so well after what you have told us that such things cannot happen again. . ." Thanks for sharing. Pride marching before the fall!

Page 39

Top. "But the actual or potential alcoholic, with hardly an exception, will *be absolutely unable to stop drinking on the basis of self-knowledge."* Knowledge isn't king against King Alcohol.

Page 40

Mid. ". . .I was confident it could not happen to me. . .I would therefore be successful where you men failed." A recipe for disaster: step one denial mixed with a generous sprinkling of pride, arrogance, and self-reliance.

Page 41

Bog. *"Not only had I been off guard, I had made no fight whatever against the first drink. This time I had not thought of the consequences at all."* Inserting Fred into the italicized lines on page 24, we have:

> *The fact is that Fred, for reasons yet obscure, has lost the power of choice in drink. His so-called will power has become practically nonexistent. He is unable, at certain times, to bring into his consciousness with sufficient force the memory of the suffering and humiliation of even a week or a month ago. Fred is without defense against the first drink.*

Page 42

Top. "I saw that will power and self-knowledge would not help in those strange mental blank spots." Hence the need to turn outside of self for a solution to the merciless obsession – "assuming, of course, that the reader desires to stop." (34)

Top. "I had never been able to understand people who said that a problem had them hopelessly defeated. I knew then." Fred discovers step one.

Bot. "It meant I would have to throw several lifelong conceptions out of the window." Again from page 14, top: "Simple, but not easy: a price had to be paid. It meant destruction of self-centeredness. I must turn in all things to the Father of Light [Steps three and eleven]. . ." Illustrative of this "turning to" is a reliance on AA in all things pertaining to one's abstinence.

☞ This "change in lifelong conceptions" is reflective of spiritual conversion. See again page 27 and Jung's treatment of Roland H.

Bot. "But the moment I made up my mind to go through with the process, I had the curious feeling that my alcoholic condition [obsession] was relieved, as in fact it proved to be." Fred, humbled and humiliated by King Alcohol, finally surrenders the management of his drinking problem to a Power greater than himself; finally works steps one, two, and three: "I can't. You can. Help me." (When the student is ready, the teacher – or AA – appears!) See also Bill's spiritual awakening in Towns Hospital. (14).

Page 43

Top. "Most alcoholics have to be pretty badly mangled before they really commence to solve their problems." Attitude elaborated upon in the *12x12*, page 24, beginning with first paragraph.

☞ The phrase *hitting bottom* does not appear in the basic text. The idea, however, is nicely captured in these few lines from the story, "It Might Have Been Worse":

> There comes a time when you don't want to live and are afraid to die. Some crisis brings you to a point of deciding to do something about your drinking problem. Try anything. Help you once continually rejected, suggestions once turned aside are finally accepted in desperation." (Second edition, 386-87)

Mid. "One of these men, staff member of a world renowned hospital . . ." Percy Polick, MD. Bellevue Hospital, New York City. (*RG*, 130)

Bot. "Once more: The alcoholic at *certain times* has no effective mental defense against the first drink." (Italics added.) The text does not appear to be arguing that the alcoholic is *always* powerless before the god alcohol; only that he cannot *consistently* rely on self-will or self-knowledge to defend him against this god.

Bot. "His defense must come from a Higher Power." Again, *power* through relationship with God or AA is being advanced as solution to *powerlessness* over one's relationship with King Alcohol. The twelve steps help facilitate the building or renewing of this vital spiritual relationship.

☞ In a letter to Bill Wilson dated January 30, 1961, Carl Jung observed: "Alcohol in Latin is *spiritus*, and you use the same word for the highest religious experience as well as for the most depraving poison. The helpful formula therefore is: *spiritus contra spiritum."* (*PIO,* 384) Roughly translated: "It takes the Spirit of God to overcome the (harmful) spirit of alcohol" (*NW*, 13)

☞ It should be noted that the alcoholic does *not* turn to AA or his Higher Power for added willpower or knowledge to resist the bottle's call; rather, he opens himself to relationship with a Power greater than himself to *remove the call* itself. As observed on page 85, "We feel as though we had been placed in a position of neutrality – safe and protected. We have not even sworn off.

Instead the problem has been removed. It does not exist for us . . . This is how we react so long as we keep in fit spiritual condition."

☞ It should also be noted that abstinence, whether for thirty days or thirty years, does not mean the absence of powerlessness. It only means the absence of alcohol.

Chapter 4

We Agnostics

Summary - Reiterates the need for *a Power* greater than oneself (God) as solution to a *power* greater than oneself (alcoholic obsession). Cautions the atheist or agnostic against being intimidated or turned off by matters spiritual of the idea of a Higher Power, and argues for the existence of a Supreme Being and the value of living by spiritual principles. Spotlights the critical role the principle of *willingness* plays in spiritual growth and development. And concludes with another account of sudden conversion and exodus from King Alcohol's mad realm.

Page 44
Top. "If, when you honestly want to. . ." Both a summary statement of allergy and obsession, and a suggested diagnosis:

> *Obsession of the mind* – If, when you honestly want to, you find you cannot quit entirely,

> *Allergy of the Body* – or if when drinking, you have little control over the amount you take,

> *Diagnosis* – you are probably alcoholic.

These two elements – *allergy and obsession* – the physical and mental dimensions of alcoholism – are implicit in the first half of step one. That is, in admitting she is powerless over alcohol, the alcoholic is admitting that:

> She cannot consistently stay away from the first drink (*obsession*),

> *and*

> she has little control over her drinking once she begins (*allergy*).

☞ It is not allergy but obsession that *brings and binds* the alcoholic to AA. What happens after the drink is of little importance – provided "our friend never [takes] the first drink, thereby setting the terrible cycle in motion." (23) But acceptance of powerlessness over obsession is acceptance that "at certain times [our friend] has no effective defense against the first drink." (43) Hence the need for a vital and *sustained* Higher Power relationship.

☞ Being powerless over alcohol does *not* mean that willpower and self-knowledge will never defend you against the first drink, or that should you drink, intoxication is a given. Rather, that you cannot consistently predict the outcome of any showdown with King Alcohol. You might walk away intact. You might have one drink, wonder what the heck you're doing, and get to a meeting right fast. Or you might have one drink and remember nothing else but waking up the next day in another state. The point is that you cannot consistently rely on your own limited resources.

Top. ". . . you *may be* suffering from an illness. . ." (Italics added.) It is essential that the reader draw her own conclusion about the drink problem. Acceptance must come from within. Trying to impose a label or diagnosis on her is a good way of inviting denial or resistance – or even defiance in the form of another bout with the bottle. This approach is equally evident in the self-diagnostic tests on pages 31 and 34, and in the text's guidelines on carrying the message in Chapter 7: "And be careful not to brand him as an alcoholic. Let him draw his own conclusion." (92)

Top. ". . . you may be suffering from an illness which only a spiritual experience will conquer." Suggested interpretation: You may be suffering from an illness that only a personality change rooted in a Higher Power relationship will help you arrest.

Mid. "To be doomed to an alcoholic death or to live on a spiritual basis are not always easy alternatives to face." The proverbial rock and a hard place. See the *12x12,* page 25.

☞ The reader may find the stuff of Chapter 4 somewhat difficult to navigate. Its objective is to help the atheist (one who maintains that the proposition, "God exists," is false) or agnostic (one who asserts that the proposition, "God exists," cannot be proven) endorse, however tentatively, the idea of a Higher Power, thus allowing them to embrace a spiritual solution to their alcohol problem. This is to be accomplished by first, suggesting various proofs for the existence of God, and second, demonstrating the value or benefits of living by spiritual principles.

The proofs given argue from the existence of various kinds of *order* – aesthetic, causal, or teleological – to the existence of a Supreme Being. Aesthetic proofs argue from the experience of beauty or splendor to the presence of a God; causal arguments postulate the existence of a Creative Intelligence to explain the orderliness or regularity of the universe (*EP,* Vol. 8; 84); and teleological proofs argue from the presence of design in the natural world to the existence of a Universal Designer. Thus on page 46 we have a variation on the aesthetic proof: "Yet, in other moments, we found ourselves thinking, when enchanted by a starlit night, 'Who, then, made all this?' There was a feeling or awe and wonder. . ." And later in the chapter we find the text appealing to both causal and teleological order to justify belief in some God:

> When, however, the perfectly logical assumption is suggested that underneath the material world and life as we see it, there is an All Powerful, Guiding, Creative Intelligence, right there our perverse streak comes to the surface and we laboriously set out to convince ourselves it isn't so. We read worldly books and indulge in windy

arguments, thinking we believe this universe needs no God to explain. (49)

While these proofs may have some intellectual or visceral appeal, especially the argument from aesthetic order (it is but a short jump from being engulfed in the splendor and stillness of the Grand Canyon, for example, to positing the existence of a Creator or Supreme Being), their ability to pass muster is another matter entirely. My concern here, however, lies not in exploring the various merits or deficiencies of these arguments, but rather in offering both rationale for their presence in the chapter – to help the atheist or agnostic hurdle the God question – and assistance in spotting them along the way.

☞ The chapter seems on much firmer ground when advocating for a God-centered or spiritually focused lifestyle. (The two are not synonymous. One can profess belief in a Supreme Being without being especially spiritual. Conversely, one can lead an especially spiritual existence while also rejecting the idea of a Judeo-Christian God.) Put simply, the text is suggesting that if the alcoholic wants to get out from under the bottle and have a go at life, then she had better stop doing what hasn't been working and start doing what has been working for those already living life:

> We used to amuse ourselves by cynically dissecting spiritual beliefs and practices when we might have observed that many spiritually-minded persons of all races, colors, and creeds were demonstrating a degree of stability, happiness and usefulness which we should have sought ourselves." (49, bottom)

Ironically, it is John Barleycorn more than anything else that readies the alcoholic to embrace a spiritual remedy for the mighty obsession: "Faced with alcoholic destruction, we soon became as open minded on spiritual matters as we had tried to be on others questions. In this respect alcohol was a great persuader." (48, top) (Alcohol as the mighty leveler of pride, rebelliousness, and puffed ego has already been observed in "Bill's Story.")

Two additional points. First the text is not arguing here for the existence of God; it is simply making the empirical claim that those who lead a Godly existence are "demonstrating a degree of stability, happiness and usefulness" not associated with those who live by self-propulsion:

> My brilliant agnosticism vanished, and I saw for the first time that those who really believed, or at least honestly tried to find a Power greater than themselves, were much more composed and contented that I had ever been, and they seemed to have a degree of happiness which I had never known. (Second edition, 247-48).

And second, Chapter 4 is not simply advocating for belief in some Power greater than self. It is also advocating for a complete overhauling of that *very* self:

> Once confused and baffled by the seeming futility of existence, they show the underlying reasons why they were making heavy going of life. *Leaving aside the drink question*, they tell why living was so unsatisfactory." (51) (Italics added.)

Ultimately, it is these underlying reasons – the reasons why living was so unsatisfactory with or without drink – that must be addressed if the alcoholic is to realize a lasting separation from the bottle.

☞ Chapter 4 makes no mention of the method of substitution, i.e., using the AA group itself as Higher Power. It does, however, appear on page 27 of the *12x12,* and find expression in these lines from Jim B's story, "The Vicious Cycle":

> For a long time the only Higher Power I could conceive was the power of the group, but this was far more than I have ever recognized before, and it was at least a beginning. It was also an ending, for never since June 16th, 1938, have I had to walk alone. (Second edition, 248)

Bot. ". . . we had to face the fact that we must find a spiritual basis of life – or else." Again, individual recovery is contingent upon aligning one's will with some power (AA) or Power (God) greater than oneself.

☞ There may be some morphing of spirituality and theism here. The two are not the same. In theory and practice, there is no contradiction in embracing the twelve steps philosophy while also rejecting the belief in a personal Supreme Being. Deliverance from the bottle seems less the function of a particular belief than it does a humble reliance on, an appealing to, something greater than self.

Page 45
Top. "Lack of power, that was our dilemma." Alternate phrasing of step one powerlessness.

Top. "We had to find a power by which we could live, and it had to be a *Power greater than ourselves.*" Power again being advanced as the solution to powerlessness. Hence step two: "Came to believe that a Power greater than ourselves could restore us to sanity [lift the obsession]." See also page 43, bottom: "The alcoholic at certain times has no effective mental defense against the first drink. . . His defense must come from a Higher Power [relationship]."

☞ Note that the text does not speak here of finding a power to lift the merciless obsession (though this is certainly implied and certainly a proper function of this Power); rather, of finding a *Power greater than ourselves* "by which we could live." The Big Book is not simply recommending a Higher Power relationship to free the alcoholic from the bottle. It is arguing the need for the alcoholic to stop living by self-propulsion and start living by God's intention for him (steps three and eleven). It is advancing the idea that the alcoholic's basic problem is less the bottle than his selfish and self-sufficient ways, ways that have closed the channel to his Higher Power – of which the bottle emerges as symbol. For sobriety to be a real option, for her obsession with intoxication to be lifted, the alcoholic must rid herself of this self-centeredness. She must open herself to a Higher Power relationship; she must relate herself rightly to her God. (*12x12; 33*)

☞ Bottle as symbol of estranged Higher Power relationship is not difficult to see. As his alcoholism progresses, as chasing the experience of intoxication becomes ever more crucial, all others and all other considerations – including his Higher Power relationship – are slowly pushed aside. King Alcohol emerges center stage. It dwarfs over and dominates. It rules.

☞ There's a cruel irony in the alcoholic's turning outside herself for rescue from the bottle, as it was to the bottle she initially turned for rescue from her woes. Questing for solution to her emotional and spiritual ills, she stumbled upon drink as universal panacea. Magic in a tonic: the freedom from and freedom to be. The good news was that it seemed to work; the bad news was that it was but an illusion. Instead of a fix there were now two problems: her initial bag of woes *and* King Alcohol. Betrayed by her own solution, imprisoned in her addictive relationship, she had "but two alternatives: One was to go on to the bitter end, blotting out the consciousness of [her] intolerable situation as best [she] could; and the other, to accept [God's or AA's] help." (25)

Mid. ". . . that's exactly what this book is about. Its main object is to enable you to find a Power greater than yourself which will solve your problem. That means we have written a book which we believe to be spiritual as well as moral. And it means, of course, that we are going to talk about God." The reader is again cautioned against throwing out the Big Book's messages of hope and deliverance with a spirituality or Higher Power concept she may find wanting. Ebby T's advice to Bill in Chapter 1 (*"Why don't you choose your own conception of God?"*) may be instructive here. "Remember we deal with alcohol – cunning, baffling, powerful! Without help it is too much for us." (58-59)

Page 46
Top. "We looked upon this world of warring individuals, warring theological systems, and inexplicable calamity, with deep skepticism . . .How could a Supreme Being have anything to do with it at all?" The problem of evil: How can one reconcile "the contradiction, or apparent contradiction, between the reality of evil [natural disasters, illness, war, cruelty and suffering] on the one hand, and religious beliefs in the goodness and power of God or of the Ultimate on the other." (*EP,* Volume 3, 136).

Top. "Yet, in other moments, we found ourselves thinking, when enchanted by a starlit night, 'Who, then, made all this?' There was a feeling of awe and wonder. . ." Aesthetic order as promoting speculation in the existence of God.

Mid. "We found that as soon as we were able to lay aside prejudice and express even a willingness to believe in a Power greater than ourselves we commenced to get results." Willingness as one of the three essentials of recovery: "We find that no one need have difficulty with the spirituality of the program. *Willingness, honesty and open mindedness are the essentials of recovery. But these are indispensable."* (Appendix II)

Bot. "Our own conception, however inadequate, was sufficient to make the approach and to effect a contact with Him." Contact as in personal *relationship.*

Page 48
Top. "Faced with alcoholic destruction, we soon became as open minded on spiritual matters as we had tried to be on other questions. In this respect alcohol was a great persuader." Same idea expressed on page 57: "Circumstances made him willing to believe"; and story, "It Might Have Been Worse": "The fact that AA is a spiritual program didn't scare me or raise any prejudice in my mind. I couldn't afford the luxury of prejudice. I had tried my way and had failed." (Second edition, 390)

Page 49
Top. ". . . the perfectly logical assumption is suggested that underneath the material world and life as we see it, there is an All Powerful, Guiding, Creative Intelligence. . ." Appeal to both causal and teleological order in arguing for the existence of God.

Bot. ". . .when we might have observed that many spiritually-minded persons of all races, colors, and creeds were demonstrating a degree of stability, happiness and usefulness which we should have sought ourselves." Similar sentiment found in "The Vicious Cycle":

> My brilliant agnosticism vanished, and I saw for the first time that those who really believed, or at least honestly tried to find a Power greater than themselves, were much more composed and contented than I had ever been, and they seemed to have a degree of happiness which I had never known." (Second edition, 247-248)

Page 50
Mid. ". . . a celebrated American statesman. . ." Alfred E. Smith (1873-1944), four time governor of New York and Democratic candidate for the presidency, 1929. (*CEO*)

Bot. "Here are thousands of men and women. . ." The first edition, first printing, reads: "Here are hundreds of men and women. . ."

Bot. ". . . there has been a revolutionary change in their way of living and thinking. Reference to spiritual conversion. Again from Chapter 2, page 25:

"The great fact is that we have had deep and effective spiritual experiences which have revolutionized our whole attitude toward life, toward our fellows and toward God's universe."

Bot. "In the face of collapse and despair, in the face of the total failure of their human resources, they found that a new power, peace, happiness, and sense of direction flowed into them." The underlying dynamic of spiritual conversion – calamity, utter defeat, and appeal to a Higher Power – as so eloquently captured in these few words by the Jungian analyst, Marion Woodman: "The god comes in through the wound." (*Parabola.* Volume XII, Number 2, May 1987). The alcoholic is licked. Overwhelmed and overmatched, he lays down his ego and cries out for help. "Help which [he] once continually rejected, suggestions once turned aside are finally accepted in desperation." ("It Might Have Been Worse"; Second edition, 386-87) King Alcohol has won; yet paradoxically, the alcoholic is about to win out. To borrow from the old saying, "When the teacher is ready, the student appears": When the alcoholic is ready, his Higher Power appears.

The reader is also referred to pages 21-22 in the *12x12* for a discussion of the paradox of strength through admission of defeat.

☞ For most, this personality change, this "new power, peace, happiness, and sense of direction," comes slowly, over time; for others, like Bill, in a loaded moment. Regardless, it is the alcoholic's own demise at the hand of King Alcohol that sets the stage for conversion. Transposing our cited line onto the text's the three pertinent ideas (60), we have:

(a) In the face of collapse and despair, (*Calamity*)
(b) In the face of the total failure of their human resources, (*Defeat*)
(c) They found that a new power, peace, happiness, and sense of direction flowed into them once they whole-heartedly sought God. (*Appeal to a Higher Power*)

- Or -

(a) In the face of collapse and despair, (*Calamity*)
(b) In the face of the total failure of their human resources, (*Defeat*),
(c) They found that a new power, peace, happiness, and sense of direction flowed into them once they appealed to AA for help. (*Appeal to a Higher Power*)

Bot. "This [spiritual change or conversion] happened soon after they met a few simple requirements." See again pages 13-14:

[Ebby] promised when these things were done [performing spiritual activities that were to be forged into the twelve steps] I would enter upon a new relationship with my Creator; that I would have the elements of a way of living which answered all my problems. Belief in the power of God, plus enough willingness, honesty and humility to establish and maintain the new order of things, were the essential requirements.

Page 51

Top. ". . . they show the underlying reasons why they were making heavy going of life. Leaving aside the drink question, they tell us why living was so unsatisfactory." The alcoholic has more than a drinking problem. He has a living problem. His cares and woes just don't begin and end with the bottle. His parading through life as his own higher power has also failed him miserably. Until and unless this is fully understood, until and unless he accepts his own role in his demise and misery, his prospects for a change in fortune are slim at best.

☞ Self-sufficiency as bankrupt philosophy is examined on pages 36-37 in the *12x12*.

Bot. "Did not Professor Langley's flying machine go to the bottom of the Potomac River?" Samuel P. Langley (1834-1906), engineer, astronomer, and secretary of the Smithsonian Institute. His assistant, Charles Manley, made two failed attempts to fly a heavier-than-air, engine-driven plane across the Potomac River in 1903. (*CEO*)

Page 52

Mid. "We had to ask ourselves why we shouldn't apply to our human problems the same readiness to change our point of view." Self-sufficiency didn't work. God-sufficiency did. The idea may be integrated into the first three steps:

> (a) Doing things my way doesn't work (*Step One*)
> (b) Doing things my Higher Power's way does work. (*Step Two*)
> (c) I'll do things my Higher Power's way. (*Step Three*)

> - Or -

> (a) My way doesn't keep me sober. (*Step One*)
> (b) AA's way keeps people sober. (Step Two)
> (c) I'll do recovery AA's way. (*Step Three*)

☞ The text is arguing from analogy. It is inviting the reader to be as open-minded and flexible in regards to matters spiritual as he or she is in regard to the material, as willing to discard spiritual dead-ends (the idea that "self-sufficiency would solve our problems") as s/he would be to "throw away the theory or gadget which does not work for something new which does." (52)

Mid. "We were having trouble with personal relationships, we couldn't control our emotional natures, we were a prey to misery and depression, we couldn't make a living, we had a feeling of uselessness, we were full of fear,

we were unhappy, we couldn't seem to be of real help to other people. . ."
Unmanageability—emotional, social, spiritual, financial, familial—gifted by
both King Alcohol and the philosophy of self-sufficiency.

. . . "was not a basic solution to these bedevilments more important than
whether we should see newsreels of lunar flight?" Suggested reading: was
not a solution to our living problems more important than clinging to biased
ideas about the ream of the spirit, or "doubting the power of God" or AA?

Bot. "Our ideas didn't work. But the God idea did." The proof is in the
pudding. Again from page 50: "This Power has in each case accomplished
the miraculous, the humanly impossible."

Page 53
Mid. "When we became alcoholics, crushed by a self-imposed crisis. . ."
What's going on here? Is the Big Book suggesting that the alcoholic's
alcoholism is, at least in part, a condition of his own making? Did he cause,
or at least contribute to, the unleashing of some power that he became
powerless to stop? If so, how does this square with the notion of fault-free
illness and "The Doctor's Opinion" and it's advocating for alcoholism as
allergy and obsession – not weakness or badness? I'm not sure that I can
provide the reader with a tidy resolution to this puzzlement, this apparent
tension in the text between shifting the locus of responsibility for the
alcoholic's illness alternately inside and outside himself. (*VS, 86-87)* But let's
have a go at it.

To begin, the idea of alcoholism as a *fault-free* illness is not found in the Big
Book. There are a host of illnesses for which individuals bear at last partial
responsibility for acquiring, and alcoholism – at least *Alcoholics Anonymous'*
understanding of it – may well be one of these. The Big Book argues that the
alcoholic's inability to control his or her drinking is rooted in illness – *not*
that the alcoholic plays no role in developing this illness. If anything, these
words from Dr. Bob certainly suggest an element of personal accountability:

> I used to get terribly upset when I saw my friends drink and knew I
> could not, but I schooled myself to believe that though I once had
> the same privilege, I had abused it so frightfully that it was
> withdrawn. So it doesn't behoove me to squawk about it for, after
> all, nobody ever had to throw me down and pour liquor down my
> throat. (Second edition, 181)

Too, the Big Book is advancing the idea of a spiritual aspect or dimension
to this malady – the problem of *self.* It is this dimension that finds expression
in the following citations:

- "Selfishness—self-centeredness. That, we think, is the root of
  our troubles." (62)
- "Our liquor was but a symptom [of being out of harmony with
  God]. (64)

- *"After all, our problems were of our own making. Bottles were only a symbol."* (103)

- "Doc [Bob] dwelt on the idea that this was an illness, but Doc was pretty frank with me. He found that I had enough faith in the Almighty to be fairly frank. He pointed out to me that probably it was more of a moral or spiritual illness than it was a physical one." ("He Thought He Could Drink Like A Gentleman," Second edition, 219)

- "I *have* learned to recognize and acknowledge the underlying cause of my disease; selfishness, self-pity and resentment [manifestations of the problem of self]." (Florence R., "A Feminine Victory," First edition, 218)

While I'm not inclined to visit these citations individually, collectively they certainly suggest a sufferer not entirely divorced from any responsibility for her suffering – assuming, of course, at least marginal responsibility for one's spiritual life.

So what are we to make of the "self-imposed crisis we could not postpone or evade"? Perhaps the self-imposed crisis is the alcoholic's alienation from her Higher Power (itself a casualty of self-will run riot or, to borrow from Mercadante's *Victims & Sinners,* self-denigration) – of which the bottle emerges as both symbol and symptom. To thus separate herself from the bottle (have the merciless obsession lifted) the text recommends a correcting of her spiritual heading and a turning back to her God. (See again Big Book Recovery, Part II, III.)

☞ The above paragraph might also be fashioned to fit the *relapse process.* That is, relapse is the process of turning from AA or one's Higher Power (itself a casualty of self-denigration or self-will run riot) – as symbolized by a re-appearance of the bottle. To thus separate oneself from the bottle – have the alcoholic obsession lifted – AA recommends a correcting of one's spiritual heading and a turning back to program, fellowship, and one's God.

Bot. "In this book you will read the experience of a man who thought he was an atheist." Fitz M, "Our Southern Friend."

Page 57
Top. "God had restored his sanity." Step two: A Power greater than Fitz had removed his alcohol obsession. "Save for a few brief moments of temptation the thought of drink has never returned; and at such times" (57) Fitz recoiled from it as from a hot flame. (84).

☞ Compare Fitz's newfound, sane response to liquor to typical pre-conversion days:

The almost certain consequences that follow taking even a glass of beer do not crowd into the mind to deter us. If these thoughts occur, they are hazy and readily supplanted with the old threadbare idea that this time we shall handle ourselves like other people. There is a complete failure of the kind of defense that keeps one from putting his hand on a hot stove. (24)

Top. "Circumstances made him willing to believe." The circumstances of both liquor and self-will run riot. (*12x12*, 38) Similar idea expressed in these lines from "It Might Have Been Worse": "The fact that A.A. is a spiritual program didn't scare me or raise any prejudice in my mind. I couldn't afford the luxury of prejudice. I had tried my way and had failed." (Second edition, 392) See also the *12x12*, 37-38.

Top. "Even so has God restored us all to our right minds." Lifted the alcohol obsession, the obsession with intoxication or controlled use.

Chapter 5

How It Works

Summary - Offers a statement of the twelve steps or directions into recovery, an introduction to the problem of "self," rationale for self-survey, and a recipe for addressing resentments. It might also be noted that nowhere in the chapter entitled "How It Works" is there to be found an account of how *it* works (though AAs might suggest that "It works quite well!"). In lieu of analysis, the text suggests action and adventure: following the same steps-directed journey out of King Alcohol's mad realm taken by AA's earliest members.

☞ Four hundred copies of the Big Book manuscript were Multilithed and circulated to members and friends of the fellowship for their comments and review. (*PIO,* 200) Various lines from this pre-publication work are cited in the study of pages 58 to 60, below. One could argue that these Multilith citations provide a truer picture of Bill's own vision of this pivotal and popular portion of the text (including the twelve steps themselves) than the consensus-driven final product. Those interested in obtaining a copy of the Multilith in its entirety are referred to the General Service Office of Alcoholics Anonymous in New York City.

☞ The accent on action over analysis seems most fitting – especially when one considers the desperate state so many alcoholics are in by the time they hit the treatment or AA doors. Put another way, if you're drowning and someone throws you a life preserver, it seems wiser to grab hold than pause to debate the physics of buoyancy.

Page 58
Top. "Rarely have we seen a person fail who has thoroughly followed our path." A popular story has Bill being asked in later years if he would make any changes to the Big Book, and replying that he would substitute the word "never" for "rarely." Bill himself denied this. (*PIO,* 200)

☞ The Multilith or pre-publication manuscript reads: "Rarely have we seen a person fail who has thoroughly followed our directions." (*M,* 26) The twelve steps as directions. See again Chapter 2, last page: "Further on, clear-cut directions are given showing how we recovered." Reference to steps as directions is also found in Chapter 6: "If we have carefully followed directions. . ." (85, bottom)

Top. "Those who do not recover are people who cannot or will not completely give themselves to this program. . ." That is people "who cannot or will not" work step three.

". . . usually men and women who are constitutionally incapable of being honest with themselves." The seeming inability to see oneself in ways so exquisitely obvious to others; the apparent inability to profit from experience or reap the lessons of one's own story

☞ It's not unusual for patients to wonder if they might be members of the class of the constitutionally incapable. (Or at least it's not unusual for *their alcoholism* to suggest this possibility to them.) Such questioning is, of course, quite self-serving, i.e., "If my constitutional incapacity rules out the possibility of personal recovery, I might as well drink." A delicious catch-22 presents itself here: Those naturally incapable of being honest with themselves are out of tune with their constitutional incapacity, for such an insight requires a degree of self-awareness that, by definition, the constitutionally incapable simply do not possess. Thus, to consider the possibility of a constitutional incapacity is to automatically rule out that very capacity. In the end, it's probably simpler just to recover.

Top. "They seem to be born that way." I'm content to let others debate the merits of this empirical (or anecdotal) claim.

Top. ". . . a manner of living which demands rigorous honesty." The Multilith reads: ". . . a way of life that demands rigorous honestly."

Mid. "There are those, too, who suffer from grave emotional and mental disorders . . ." One such person was Bill Wilson, whose bouts of depression, beginning at the age 10 or 11 following the separation of his parents, would continue into his adulthood and recovery from alcoholism. (*PIO*, 24-25, 292-303)

☞ Alcoholics may occasionally find themselves pressured by sponsors or other AAs into refusing or discontinuing medication for the treatment of a mental illness. The purported thinking of these AAs is that pharmacological intervention is either unnecessary ("You don't need medication; you just need to work a better program."), or compromises the letter or spirit of abstinence. Ironically, such thinking issues from the same "world of ignorance and misunderstanding" (20) that prescribes willpower as an antidote to a drinking problem. It also flies in the face of the Big Book's own words on seeking professional help for mental health concerns:

> God has abundantly supplied this world with fine doctors, psychologists, and practitioners of various kinds. Do not hesitate to take your health problems to such persons . . . Try to remember that though God has wrought miracles among us, we should never belittle a good doctor or psychiatrist. Their services are often indispensable in treating a newcomer and in following his case afterward. (133)

Interested readers are also encouraged to obtain the pamphlet, "The A.A. Member – Medications and Other Drug," available at many treatment center bookstores or AA intergroup offices, or through A.A. World Services, Inc.

Mid. "If you have decided you want what we have and are willing to go to any length to get it . . ." *Step zero* as necessary condition for recovery. Again from page 34: "We are assuming, of course, that the reader desires to stop [drinking]."

". . . then you are ready to take certain steps." The Multilith reads: ". . . then you are ready to follow directions."

Bot. "At some of these we balked. We thought we could find an easier, softer way. But we could not." Multilith reads: "At some of these you may balk. You may think you can find an easier, softer way. We doubt if you can." (*M*, 26) The pronoun shift – from *you* to *we* – is significant for several reasons. First, it permits the reader or practicing alcoholic the dignity of deciding for herself whether she can "find an easier, softer way." Second, it reduces the risk of engaging the alcoholic's defiance ("What do you mean *I* can't find an easier, softer way? *I'll* show you!"), thus alienating the very people the fellowship wishes to support. And third, it's consistent with the notion of recovery as rooted in the sharing of one's experience, strength and hope. This pronoun change will be observed in other Multilith passages that follow.

Bot. "Remember that we deal with alcohol – cunning, baffling . . ." From Chapter 3: "This is the baffling feature of alcoholism as we know it – this utter inability to leave it alone, no matter how great the necessity or the wish."

☞ The Multilith reads: "Remember that you are dealing with alcohol – cunning, baffling, powerful! Without help it is too much for you." (*M*, 26) Again, language that might well turn off the very reader the fellowship wishes to engage.

Page 59
Top. "Without help it is too much for us." From page 45: "Lack of power, that was our dilemma."

Top. "But there is One who has all power – that One is God. May you find Him now!" Again from page 45: "We had to find a power by which we could live, and it had to be a *Power greater than ourselves.*"

☞ The Multilith reads: "But there is One who has all power – That one is God. You must find Him now!" (*M*, 26)

☞ The reader is again cautioned against losing sight of the Big Book's message of hope and deliverance in a tussle over a belief system she may find wanting. Remember: It's *your* Higher Power as *you* understand it. If you don't or can't embrace the idea of a personal God, consider using the AA group or fellowship itself as Higher Power. *"The main thing is that [you] be willing to believe in a Power greater than [yourself] and that [you] live by spiritual principles."* (93)

Top. "Half measures availed us nothing. We stood at the turning point. We asked His protection and care with complete abandon." Surrender.

☞ The Multilith reads: "Half measures will avail you nothing. You stand at the turning point. Throw yourself under His protection and care with complete abandon."

☞ Crisis of self-surrender also expressed in these lines from page 25:

> If you are as seriously alcoholic as we were, we believe there is no middle-of-the-road solution. We were in a position where life was becoming impossible, and if we had passed into the region from which there is no return through human aid, we had but two alternatives: One was to go on to the bitter end . . ; and the other, to accept spiritual help.

And from Shoemaker's *Realizing Religion:*

> William James speaks with great emphasis upon this crisis of self-surrender. He says that it is "the throwing of our conscious selves on the mercy of powers which, whatever they may be, are more ideal than we are actually, and make for our redemption . . . Self-surrender has always been and always must be regarded as the vital turning-point of the religious life, so far as the religious life is spiritual and no affair of outer works and ritual and sacrament . . ." (OGAA, 137)

Top. "Here are the steps we took, which are suggested as a program of recovery." Written by Bill while lying in bed at his home in Brooklyn (*PIO,* 197), the twelve steps were an elaboration of the six-step program that he had been working ever since his own recovery. It was heavy with Oxford Group principles, as well as ideas borrowed from William James and Dr. Silkworth. (*PIO,* 197) As cited in Earl T's story, "He Sold Himself Short," they were:

   1. Complete deflation.
   2. Dependence and guidance from a Higher Power.
   3. Moral Inventory
   4. Confession
   5. Restitution
   6. Continued work with other alcoholics.

In listing "the steps we took," I have also provided the Multilith's wording - "M" - whenever it differs from the step itself.

   1. We admitted we were powerless over alcohol – that our lives had become unmanageable.
   M. Admitted we were powerless over alcohol – that our lives had become unmanageable.

☞ It's not uncommon for patients to mistake the completion of their step one work (assignments) for completing their working of step one, i.e., "I've finished step one." "I've got step one." "I've done step one, I'm now on two." While such thinking is understandable, especially for folks run through the task-oriented process of some treatment centers, it's not only incorrect but also hazardous to lasting sobriety. In reality, step one is *not* something we get or complete. Rather, it is a spiritual activity or exercise we continue to perform; a truth we continue to return ourselves to. **Remember: step one is not something you get; it's something you work.**

☞ Several *spiritual truths* reveal themselves to the alcoholic in working step one: She is *not* God, perfect, or self-sufficient, but a limited, imperfect being. Alcoholics have neither monopoly on, nor special claim to, these truths. They are wired into the being, human. Nor do alcoholics come to these truths out of any special virtue. Most who embrace them do so without having been run over the by the bottle. In reality, acceptance of powerlessness is less *the end* of working step one than *a gateway* to confronting one's essential finiteness. Again from "Bill's Story, "I admitted for the first time that of myself I was nothing; that without Him I was lost." (13)

☞ It is not the counselors, therapists or peers in treatment, nor the sponsors or fellow drunks around the twelve-step tables, that reveal the many truths of step one to the alcoholic. Rather, it is her story. Her story illuminates the contents of step one: not just her powerlessness and unmanageability, but a failed spiritual heading, an attempt to find deliverance from her pain, her emptiness, and her story through relationship with a drug – a *thing*. It is here, in defeat, that the alcoholic surrenders both bottle and self-sufficiency; and here, too, that she finds the willingness to consider an alternate way of living her life. To borrow from "It Might Have Been Worse":

> There comes a time when you don't want to live and are afraid to die. Some crisis brings you to a point of making a decision to do something about your drinking problem. Try anything. Help which you once continually rejected, suggestions once turned aside are finally accepted in desperation. (Second edition, 386-87)

☞ A distinction is sometimes made between admitting and accepting. For example, "I admit that I'm an alcoholic, though I've yet to accept it." Within the context of step one, however, this seems a distinction without a difference. To admit is to accept is to embrace is to "fully concede to our innermost selves that we were alcoholics. This is the first step in recovery." (30) After all, it's unlikely that Bill W. had the following in mind when considering the first step taken: We admitted we were powerless over alcohol, though not all of us accepted this – that our lives had become unmanageable, though not all of us accepted this, either.

☞ Other than found in the statement of step one on page 59, the word "unmanageable" does not appear in the recovery portion of the book. That said, there are two general types of unmanageability – alcohol and abstinence-based – with abstinence-based linked directly to the problem of *self.* To illustrate:

Andy and Barney's families arise early on a sunny, summer morn for a fun-filled day at the beach. They all enjoy hearty breakfasts; then load themselves and their laughter, beverages and treats, and beach gear and family dogs into their cars. Good cheer quickly ends, however, when neither Andy nor Barney are able to start their cars.

Considering his next move, Andy happens to catch the eye of his neighbor – and Mayberry's crackerjack mechanic, Thelma Lou – walking his way. "TL" offers a helping hand; Andy gladly accepts. In no time at all his car is purring like new, and Andy's gang is again on its way to surf and sand.

Barney, however, scoffs at Andy's surrender. Tethered to *self* – pride, prejudice and self-reliance – he's not about to concede any ground to a female mechanic (let alone one he thinks overcharged him for a tune-up two years back). Despite the pleas of wife and children, Barney stands firm and shouts his intent to "fix the damn car myself."

Four hours pass. Andy's family returns home, a rollicking good time had by all. Barney remains bent over the engine well of his car; grease and grime cover his face and hands; tools and auto parts litter his front yard. His kids have been fighting; his wife has been nagging; the family dog has run away. Unmanageability, straight up!

In this little scenario, the problem is not an uncooperative car engine. It's an uncooperative Barney. Yoked to pride, prejudice, and self-sufficiency, Barney is simply unable to take hold of his neighbor's helping hand.

☞ The wording of step one is somewhat misleading in that it suggests our lives were (or at least may have been) manageable before the reign of King Alcohol, i.e., if our lives *had become* unmanageable, it's reasonable to assume that at some time our lives *had been* manageable. In truth, however, our lives were *never* manageable (indeed, many an alcoholic's initial adventure with the bottle was itself an attempt to manage her not-in-control-ness). Nor will our lives ever be manageable – regardless of years abstinent or time spent around the AA tables. Perfection is simply beyond the reach of essentially finite beings. Instead of aiming for manageability, it may be preferable to aim for *less un*manageability.

2. Came to believe that a Power greater than ourselves could restore us to sanity.

☞ The restoration to sanity is both the lifting of the alcoholic obsession – either obsession with control (this time will be different, this time I will be able to control my intake or behavior) or with intoxication itself. Thus, from page 60, line (c): ". . . God could and would [relieve us of the alcoholic obsession] if He were sought." Also from Chapter 6, page 84:

And we have ceased fighting anything or anyone – even alcohol. For by this time *sanity* will have returned. We will seldom be interested in liquor. If tempted, we recoil from it as from a hot flame. We react sanely and normally . . . We feel as though we had been placed in a position of neutrality – safe and protected. We have not even sworn off. Instead, the [obsession] has been removed. It does not exist for us. (Italics added.)

3. **Made a decision to turn our will and our lives over to the care of God *as we understood Him.***
   M. Made a decision to turn our will and our lives over to the care and direction of God as we understood Him.

☞ The wording of step three lends itself to some confusion. Taken literally, it certainly suggests a decision to give up or surrender one's will to a Higher Power – leaving one without will or willpower, and walking about in a zombie-like state. In reality, step three is *not* a decision to rid oneself of some *thing,* but a decision to align one's will with *Something's* plan for us. Thus, step three might be understood: made a decision to bring our will into agreement with AA's treatment plan for our alcohol problem by attending meetings, working the twelve steps, connecting with fellowship, etc. (Each of these activities, of course, requires an act of will.)

☞ The qualifying phrase, "God *as we understood Him,*" signaled a compromise between the pietistic and the less religious or secular factions of AA – the former arguing that the book be laced with Christian doctrines and Biblical terms and expressions, the latter wishing to downplay references to God in both the text and steps. (*PIO,* 199) Bill himself regarded this compromise as:

> something being created that blended the finest qualities of the opposing views.
>
> First was the idea that they should always label their steps a *Suggested* Program of Recovery. Bill called this one a ten strike. They all agreed that no drunk would rebel at a mere suggestion.
>
> The next point – and this turned out to be providential – was that whenever the world 'God' was used in their literature, it should be followed by the phrase 'as we understand Him.' Bill saw that those italicized words would not only widen the gateway so that all drunks could pass through, regardless of their belief or lack of belief. In time they might also force many men to come to terms with what they understood God to be, with what it was in their lives that they truly believed it. (*BW,* 254-55)

Reference to the qualifying phrase is also found in Jim B's story, "The Vicious Cycle":

I don't think the boys were completely convinced of my personality change, for they fought shy of including my story in the book, so my only contribution to their literary efforts was my firm conviction – since I was still a theological rebel—that the word God should be qualified with the phrase "as we understand Him" – for that was the only way I could accept spirituality. (Second edition, 248)

☞ It is important to understand that step three speaks of an *ongoing* decision to let go of one's "little plans and designs" (63) – *not* a single act of surrender; of a "continual renewal" of the decision to, for example, let go of one's own ideas about the management of the alcohol problem in favor AA's ideas about the management of the problem. (*12x12*, 35)   As observed by Joe D. in his story, "The European Drinker":

That day I gave my will to God and asked to be directed. But I have never thought of that as something to do and then forget about. I very early came to see that there had to be a continual renewal of that simple deal with God; that I had perpetually to keep the bargain. So I began to pray; to place my problems in God's hands. (Second edition, 237)

It should also be noted that the *demonstration* of the third step decision lies in the *action*. For instance, the demonstration of the decision to turn the treatment of one's dental care over to the dentist lies in doing what the dentist recommends for the management of one's dental care. If the dentist recommends doing x, and x is not done, then nothing has been turned over (and the original problem likely persists or returns).

☞ Clients occasionally ask, "When will we be ready to begin making our own decisions?" I try to point out that the step three decision is *their* own decision; that in turning their alcohol problem over to AA or their will and their lives over to the care of a Higher Power, it is *they* who are doing the choosing – *not* their counselor, peers, sponsor, or God. I also remind them that recovery permits them this choosing, whereas addiction hijacks their will and does the choosing for them. (That said, I suspect what some folks really want to know is <u>not</u> when they will be ready to make their own decisions, but when they will be ready to do their *own thing.* My response: anytime you want. Just keep in mind: doing your own thing contributed mightily to your being where you are today. So, while doing your own thing is an option, do you really want to exercise it?)

☞ The reader may wonder, "Why am I turning the whole kit and caboodle over to some Higher Power – even conceding my defeat at the hands of King Alcohol *and* my belief that this Higher Power can defend against the King's bottles? I mean, I don't turn my will and my life over to the dentist for a pretty smile. I only let go of trying to manage my oral hygiene by myself. The rest of my will and my life stays with me. And I don't turn my will and my life over to the accountant to keep the revenue agent off my back. I only let go of trying to do my taxes and interpret the tax code by myself. The rest of my will and life stays with me. And even insofar as my drinking problem goes, I'm only turning the management of *that* problem over to AA. It doesn't seek custody of my will or my life, either. Why couldn't step three simply read: 'Made a decision to turn the management of my alcohol problem over to the care of a Higher Power?' By what logic do you go from surrendering control of the bottle to God to surrendering my entire will and life to God? Seems a bit sneaky and underhanded to me!"

Well, my best response – not necessary the correct response (assuming there is one) – but my best response is as follows: In *Alcoholics Anonymous,* the bottle emerges as a symbol and/or symptom of living out of relationship with one's God. Hence, if you wish to remove the bottle from the center of your life, you need to move your God into the center in your life (both can't occupy center stage at the same time). How is move accomplished? The twelve steps, especially one through seven, and ten, eleven and twelve. (See also Part II – "Bottles Were Only a Symbol").

Looking at the above through secular lenses leaves us with something like this: the presence (or return) of the bottle in the center of one's life indicates the absence of fellowship in the center of one's life. (you simply can't be lit up and tight with fellowship at the same time). Recovery, then, involves a turning to rich relations – *not* bottles or things – for comfort, guidance, and support; while relapse is a falling out of connection with kind, and resuming connection with things. Which is all a way of saying: in relapse, the bottle emerges as symbol and/or symptom of being out of relationship with kin and kind. **(This seems to dovetail with the idea of addiction as an intimacy disorder. See Appendix C.)**

4. **Made a searching and fearless moral inventory of ourselves.**

5. **Admitted to God, to ourselves, and to another human being the exact nature of our wrongs.**

6. **Were entirely ready to have God remove all these defects of character.**
   M. Were entirely willing that God remove all these defects of character.

7. **Humbly asked Him to remove our shortcomings.**
   M. Humbly, on our knees, asked Him to remove our shortcomings – *holding nothing back.*

☞ "... on our knees ..." A common practice in the Oxford Group, as found in Earl T's story, "He Sold Himself Short":

> Dr. Bob led me through all of these steps. At the moral inventory, he brought up several of my bad personality traits or character defects ... We went over these at great length, and then he finally

asked me if I wanted these defects of character removed. When I said yes, we both knelt at his desk and prayed, each of us asking to have these defects taken away. (Second edition, 292)

☞ The phrase, *"holding nothing back,"* may be derivative of Absolute Honesty, one of the Oxford Group's Four Absolutes (the others were Purity, Unselfishness, and Love). They were regarded as the standards laid down by Jesus in his Sermon on the Mount (*OGAA, 35*-37), and a suggested set of ideals against which one might make a personal inventory. (*OOGA,* 156) They are still referred to in AA groups in the Akron and Cleveland areas.

8. **Made a list of all persons we had harmed, and became willing to make amends to them all.**

9. **Made direct amends to such people wherever possible, except when to do so would injure them or others.**

10. **Continued to take personal inventory and when we were wrong promptly admitted it.**

11. **Sought through prayer and meditation to improve our conscious contact with God *as we understood Him,* praying only for knowledge of His will for us and the power to carry that out.**
   M. Sought through prayer and meditation to improve our contact with God, praying only for knowledge of his will for us and the power to carry that out.

☞ How might the atheist work step eleven? How to seek conscious contact with what *is not?* Perhaps by devoting oneself to seeking connection what *is:* the blimps on the "radar" we choose to ignore; the needs and challenges and values that beg for our attention; and the unfinished business that won't resolve itself, that is there with us as we lay our head on the pillow at night, and greets us as we rub the sleepy bugs from our eyes in the morn. To work at bringing our lives into alignment with these truths and matters seems indeed the stuff and challenge of step eleven.

12. **Having had a spiritual awakening as the result of these steps, we tried to carry this message to alcoholics, and to practice these principles in all our affairs.**
   M. Having had a spiritual experience as the result of this course of action, we tried to carry this message to others, especially alcoholics, and to practice these principles in all our affairs.

☞ "Having had a spiritual experience . . . " While a spiritual experience is "the result of these steps," it need not be the case that awakenings are experienced *only* after a formal working of the *entire steps menu* (let alone after *the first* working of these steps). In both theory and practice, spiritual experiences can occur at any time along the steps guided journey. For instance, at her first AA meeting an alcoholic realizes that she is not alone, that others share her defeat at the hands of King Alcohol, and that a life free of the merciless obsession is hers, too, for the working. Her passage from alienation to fellowship, fear to faith, despair to hope, denial to acceptance, and worry to serenity (*PTP*, xi) are the very stuff of awakenings or conversion experience. Thus, from Marty Mann's story, "Women Suffer Too":

> I went trembling into a house in Brooklyn filled with strangers . . . and I found I had come home at last, to my own kind. There is another meaning for the Hebrew word that in the King James version of the Bible is translated "salvation." It is: "to come home." I had found my salvation. I wasn't alone anymore. (Second edition, 228. Interesting aside: The house in Brooklyn was Bill and Lois Wilson's residence at 182 Clinton Street.)

☞ See discussion of "psychic change" beginning page 44 of study guide for additional comments on spiritual experience.

☞ ". . . we tried to carry this messages to others. . ." See mid-paragraph, page 25.

☞ ". . . and practice these principles in all our affairs." There is no graduation day in recovery; no end to working the steps; no moment in which it can be said, "I've arrived!"

☞ Perhaps the simplest way to regard the twelve steps is as a series of *directions* – directions leading a spent soul out of King Alcohol's "mad realm" to a spiritual experience or "personality change sufficient to bring about recovery." (569) Transposing this notion of directed journey onto the steps themselves, we have:

1. We admitted we were without defense against the first drink. (43)

2. Came to believe that a Higher Power relationship could and would provide such a defense.

3. Made a decision to develop this relationship.

4. Inventoried obstacles to this relationship.

5. Admitted to our obstacles.

6. Were ready to seek help in removing them.

7. Asked for help in removing them.

8. Made a list of persons we had harmed, and became willing to

change for the better our relationships with them.

9. Worked to change for the better our relationships with these people, except when to do so would harm them or others.
10. Continued to inventory our obstacles to recovery, and when they arose promptly dealt with them.

11. Sought to improve our Higher Power relationship; sought to know and do our Higher Power's will for us.

12. Having had a personality change sufficient to bring about recovery, we tried to carry the message to alcoholics that a Higher Power relationship had done for us what we could not do alone, and to let the twelve steps guide us in our daily affairs.

Note that in this interpretation each step speaks of a *relationship*: a relationship with self, others, community, or Higher Power. Recovery is about the building or renewing of these relationships (*AP*, 21-23), and the twelve steps guide (or direct) the spiritual traveler on this life venture. (Acceptance of powerlessness is less *the end* of working step one than *a gateway* to confronting the need for others, for connections with people – *not* things.)

Page 60
Top. "No one among us has been able to maintain anything like perfect adherence to these principles." Some folks have taken to drawing a distinction between principles and steps and offering a one-to-one correspondence between them. A popular pairing is cited by Pittman in *Practice These Principles* (xii):

Step One	Honesty
Step Two	Hope
Step Three	Faith
Step Four	Courage
Step Five	Integrity
Step Six	Willingness
Step Seven	Humility
Step Eight	Brotherly Love
Step Nine	Justice
Step Ten	Perseverance
Step Eleven	Spiritual Awareness
Step Twelve	Service

I believe this schema is incorrect. It seems evident from a reading of the paragraph that "these principles" refer directly to the preceding twelve steps (as does the word "principles" in step twelve refer to steps one to eleven and twelve itself). To suggest otherwise is to posit a group of values or virtues not enumerated anywhere in the text. The Big Book may be difficult; it's not intended as mysterious or arcane. The last thing the newcomer needs is the challenge of foraging in the spiritual ether for a set of principles to help rid her of the merciless obsession.

And even if one did acquiesce to this suggested separation of principles and steps and allow for some sort of pairing between them, the effort to establish a one-to-one correspondence seems a bit simplistic. For example, step one is as much about acceptance and humility as it is self-honesty. And step three seems equally at home with the virtues of humility and surrender as it does faith.

Perhaps instead we might consider the twelve steps as a group of spiritual exercise or activities, and allow that a sustained effort at working them will reward the practitioner with any number of spiritual gifts. For example, a regular working of step one will help promote self-acceptance, honesty and humility; while a routine working of step nine might promote self-awareness, camaraderie, and justice.

Top. "We claim spiritual progress rather than spiritual perfection." Not license for irresponsibility or non-performance, but a simple reminder of one of the essential truths revealed in the working of step one: the alcoholic is *human* – not perfect or God. Mistakes, wrongs, and wrongdoing are inevitable – not out of deficiency, but out of what it is to be human. Indeed, step ten exists to help net the endless droppings of one's humanity.

Mid. ". . . make clear three pertinent ideas:

   (a) That we were alcoholic and could not manage our own lives.
   (b) That probably no human power could have relieved our alcoholism.
   (c) That God could and would if He were sought."

Possible interpretation:

   (a) That we were powerless over alcohol. (*Step one*)
   (b) That we could not relieve ourselves of our destructive obsession. (*Step one*)
   (c) That God could and would relieve us of our obsession if we developed a relationship with God. (*Step two*)

   - Or -

   (c) That participation in AA program and fellowship could and would relieve us of our obsession. (*Step two*)

It is through this seeking, this appealing to a Power greater than herself, that the alcoholic begins to forge a spiritual relationship that helps quiet and lift the merciless obsession. (Of course, the alcoholic is not going to make this appeal, even if she regards AA favorably, until first admitting that she is powerless over alcohol—that her life has become unmanageable. No admitted defeat, no incentive to reach beyond her limited resources for rescue from the bottle.)

☞ The Multilith includes these words following three pertinent ideas: "If you are not convinced on these vital issues, you ought to re-read the book to this point or else throw it away!"

Another option is found on the inside rear dust jacket of the first edition:

> This book may be ordered from the publisher upon a free examination basis. Send $3.50 or instruct to send C.O.D. and pay the few extra cents money return cost. Examine for seven days and if not satisfied that the book will be helpful return and money (including postage) will be refunded. (Tenth printing)

Bot. "Being convinced . . ." That is, being convinced of the three pertinent ideas, being convinced of steps one and two.

Bot. "Just what do we mean by [turning our will and our life over to God as we understand Him], and just what do we do?" The first thing we do – the first requirement for working step three – "is to be convinced that any life run on self-will can hardly be a success." (60) As the first requirement for turning his alcohol problem over to AA is to be convinced that he is unable to manage his own drinking (step one), so too the first requirement for turning his will and his life over to a Higher Power is to be convinced that doing things his way (the philosophy of self-sufficiency) has not been working – again step one. (See also the *12x12,* 37 to 38, top.)

☞ The reader may still wonder why she must surrender both the bottle *and* her will and her life to a Power greater than herself? Why is it not sufficient to let AA manage her alcoholism while still maintaining rule over the rest of her domain? By what logic or reasoning, she might ask, does one move from step one (admission of powerlessness over alcohol) to step three (turning the whole kit and caboodle over to some Higher Power)? The answer, I believe, has to do with the very nature of the bottle itself: in *Alcoholics Anonymous,* the bottle emerges as *symbol* of *living out of relationship* with one's God, as symptom of a life directed toward satisfying *my* little "plans and designs" – *not* my Higher Power's design for me. Thus wondering, "Why can't I let my Higher Power manage my alcohol dependence while I direct the rest of the show?" seems but a variation on having one's cake and eating it too. (See also discussion of step three, above.)

Bot. "Each person is like an actor who wants to run the whole show . . ." The actor is not content with his role. He oversteps his bounds. He attempts to play God. Problems of his own making – self-bred unmanageability – ensue.

Page 61

Mid. "He becomes angry, indignant, self-pitying." Abstinence-based un-manageability. Contrast with post-surrender days:

> We are then in much less danger of excitement, fear, anger, worry, self-pity, or foolish decisions. We become much more efficient. We do not tire so easily, for we are not burning up energy foolishly as we did when we were trying to arrange life to suit ourselves. (88)

Page 62

Top. "Selfishness—self-centeredness. That, we think, is the root of our troubles." The spiritual root of the alcoholic's woes, *including* his tussle with the bottle (see again Big Book Recovery Philosophy, Parts II and III, and study of Chapter 4). The problem of *self* is somewhat difficult to define. It is not simply raw ego or willfulness, fear or resentment, dishonesty or self-centeredness. It is not specific to gender, a Western notion, or a dated idea. It is whatever frustrates spiritual growth; whatever clogs one's channel to his God; whatever calls her away from the call of her better angels. It may be shame, laziness or rebelliousness, pride or prejudice, or attachment to a skewed self-portrait; or it may be craving the latest fashion, resistance to a better idea, or a need to look good for the neighbors. Self saps our energy, limits our options, and corrodes our spirit. And an alcoholic in its grip is unmanageability waiting to happen.

☞ It is important to understand that the problem of self does *not* disappear with the bottle. To the contrary, its presence and power are all the more evident in the bottle's absence. (Or as the bottle might say, "Can't point the finger at me anymore!)

☞ Selfishness—self-centeredness as a life directed to realizing one's little plans and designs (63, top) is to be distinguished from a God-centered life or a life directed to "praying only for the knowledge of [God's] will for us and the power to carry that out." Thus from page 85: "Every day is a day when we must carry the vision of God's will into all of our activities. 'How can I best serve Thee – They will (not mine) be done.'" (See also the *12x12,* page 40.)

Mid. "So our troubles, we think, are basically of our own making." To borrow from the 1970 *Pogo* cartoon, "We have met the enemy and he is us." Additional references to self-inflicted unmanageability are found on page 103: *"After all, our problems were of our own making. Bottles were only a symbol";* and 133, top: "But it is clear that we made our own misery. God didn't do it."

Mid. "Above everything, we alcoholics must be rid of this selfishness. We must or it kills us!" The problem of self as both spiritual dimension of one's alcoholism and block to God's grace.

Mid. ". . . there often seems no way of entirely getting rid of self without His aid." As the alcoholic must appeal to a Power greater than herself for rescue from the bottle (see again last paragraph page 43), so too must she turn outside herself for help in removing whatever stands between her and her God (see the Third Step Prayer on page 63 and the Seventh Step Prayer on 76; also page 71).

Bot. "Next, we decided that hereafter in this drama of life, God was going to be our Director. He is the Principal; we are His agents. He is the Father, and we are His children." The patriarchal concept of Higher Power seems at odds with the spirit of "God *as we understood Him.*" See study of page 19, bottom.

Page 63
Top. "When we sincerely took such a position . . ." That is, when we made a decision to Let Go and Let God.

". . . all sorts of remarkable things followed." Personality change or spiritual conversion: "We were reborn."

Mid. "We were now at Step Three." Not a one-time decision to direct one's will to God (or surrender one's bottle to AA), but a decision that must be repeatedly renewed. As observed by Joe D., "The European Drinker":

> That day I gave my will to God and asked to be directed. But I have never thought of that as something to do and then forget about. I very early came to see that there had to be a continual renewal of that simple deal with God; that I had perpetually to keep the bargain. So I began to pray; to place my problems in God's hand. (Second edition, 237)

Mid. "Relieve me of the bondage of self, that I may better do Thy will." Not relieve me of the bondage of self so that I may be turned into a non-entity, a hole in a donut (*12x12, 36*). But relieve me of the spiritual dimension of my illness so that I may be free of the bottle and chain; relieve me of my shortcomings, my cravings and attachments, so that I may cease being *driven and blinded* by them.

☞ A variation on the Third Step Prayer is found in Fitz M's story, "Our Southern Friend": "The thing I do is to say, 'God here I am and here are all my troubles. I've made a mess of things and can't do anything about it. You take me, and all my troubles, and do anything you want with me.'" (Second edition, 467)

Mid. "Take away my difficulties, that victory over them may bear witness to those I would help of Thy Power, Thy Love, and Thy Way of Life." Witnessing for God. Alternatively, one might witness for AA: "Take away my [drinking problem], that victory over [the obsession] may bear witness to those I would" help of AA's solution for them.

Mid. "We thought well before taking this step making sure we were ready; that we could at last abandon ourselves utterly to Him." Remember: "No one among us has been able to maintain anything like perfect adherence to these principles. We are not saints." (60)

Bot. "Next we launched out on a course of vigorous action . . ." Again, the *demonstration* of the step three decision to turn one's will and one's life over to the care of God (or one's drinking problem over to the management of AA) is in the *action.*

" . . . the first step of which is a personal housecleaning." Not inventory of one's family, neighbors or the world (the type for which most alcoholics are notorious), but inventory of one's self and one's own backyard.

Page 64
Top. "Though our decision was a vital and crucial step. . ." Step three.

". . . it could have little permanent effect unless at once followed by a strenuous effort to face, and to be rid of, the things in ourselves which had been blocking us." Manifestations of the problem of self as blocking us from God or God's will for us.

Top. "Our liquor was but a symptom." The bottle as a symptom of spiritual illness or estrangement from one's Higher Power.

☞ Alcoholics obviously have no monopoly on self-will. Why then their lot to have the illness of alcoholism? The book suggests the added factors of physical allergy and acquired mental obsession.

Top. "So we had to get down to causes and conditions." We had to inventory the whys of our alienation from God *and* community, others, and the world about us.

☞ While the text fingers willfulness and egregious pride as the spiritual culprits behind the alcoholic's failed spiritual heading, this needn't be so. As Linda Mercadante observes in *Victims & Sinners:*

> 'Self-will run riot' is by far not the only way to turn from God. (39). Sin [not moral, but religious: living out of relationship with one's God] can be two-sided. One need not sin only through self-elevation; one can sin also through inordinate self-abnegation or denigration, as women have generally been led to do. I have called this "the sin of self-loss." One can fall into ungodly despair through refusing to be a full self as much as through defiantly trying to assume Godlike proportion. This sin of sloth can be equally destructive in prompting alienation from God.

The sin of self-loss is equally important and equally damaging as inordinate pride. It is equally able to alienate one from God, self, and others and to cripple one's true potential as image of God (*imago dei*) . . . An entire audience is left unaddressed when the traditional focus on sin as inordinate self-will is stressed. Women and other disempowered people are then implicitly assisted in the sin of inordinate self-loss. They may also be blamed for succumbing to oppression. In either case, they experience further guilt and shame, rather than forgiveness and acceptance. This happens as their legitimate efforts to actualize the self are both punished by society and further discouraged through one-sided preaching against pride. Consequently, the real sin of self-loss is not addressed. It cannot be confronted, confessed, or touched with the message of divine forgiveness. (*VS,* 148-49)

Mid. "One object is to disclose damaged or unsalable goods. . ." The Big Book's self-survey focuses on obstacles to recovery – the spiritual sludge that blocks one off from her God, *as well as* herself, others, and the world about her. Logically, of course, there is no reason why inventory taking must be done in red-ink. A "fact-finding and fact-facing" survey of resources for forging a relationship with AA and one's Higher Power also has its place. Indeed, a fourth step drowning in flaws and faults, a distorted survey of past and person, is itself an obstacle to serenity and sobriety.

Mid. "Being convinced that self, manifested in various ways, was what had defeated us, we considered its common manifestations." Again, selfishness—self-centeredness, the spiritual dimension of one's illness, as "the root our problems."

☞ *Self* as block to Higher Power relationship (or relations with AA, community, and others) has its roots in the Oxford Group, with selfishness, dishonesty, resentment, and fear regarded as its most common and objectionable manifestations. (*OGAA,* 303) This heritage is also evident in the text's exploration of step ten on page 84: "Continue to watch for selfishness, dishonesty, resentment, and fear."

Bot. "Resentment is the number one offender. It destroys more alcoholics than anything else." The reliving or re-feeling of slights, hurts or wrongs – real or fancied – as number one block to God's grace:

. . . with the alcoholic, whose hope is the maintenance and growth of a spiritual experience, this business of resentment is infinitely grave. . .for when harboring such feelings we shut ourselves off from the sunlight of the Spirit. The insanity of alcohol returns [again, the bottle as both symbol and symptom of being blocked off from one's Higher Power] and we drink again. And with us, to drink is to die. (66)

Resentment as manifesting estrangement from one's Higher Power is also expressed in these fine words from "The European Drinker": "And when I get upset, cross-grained and out of tune with my fellow man I know that I am out of tune with God." (Second edition, 237)

☞ Resentment as common manifestation of self may require a little explanation. The Big Book *appears* to be arguing as follows: In living by self-propulsion, in seeking to "wrest satisfaction and happiness out of this world" (61) by "trying to arrange the lights, the ballet, the scenery, and the rest of the players (60) – in short, by trying to play God – "we step on the toes of our fellows and they retaliate." (62) Thus "[resentments], we think, are basically of our own making. They arise out of ourselves, and the alcoholic is an extreme example of self-will run riot, though he usually doesn't think so." (62) Put another way, while the alcoholic is often victimized by his resentments, he is less often an innocent in their creation.

Bot. "From it [resentment] stem all forms of spiritual disease. . ." Estrangement or alienation from one's Higher Power, *as well as* oneself, others, and the world.

Page 65
Top. "On our grudge list we set opposite each name our injuries." Easier said than done, as resentments tend to direct one outward and away from self-survey toward the wrong or wrongdoing of others. Completing columns one and two (*"I'm resentful at"* and *"The Cause,"* respectively) is relatively easy; moving beyond these into column three (*"Affects my"*) often requires courage and perseverance.

Page 66
Top. "To conclude that others were wrong was as far as most of us ever got." Most of us stayed stuck in our resentments: never venturing beyond the first and second columns of the template on page 65; deriving what mileage we could from these spiritual pests (including self-righteous indignation, character assassination, and justification to drink); neglecting to look at our own role in their creation; avoiding responsibility for putting them to sleep; and setting ourselves up for yet more turmoil in speaking ill of, or retaliating against, our wrongdoers.

Bot. "We saw that these resentments must be mastered, but how? We could not wish them away any more than alcohol." I'd like to suggest three strategies for resentment resolution: *assertiveness, prayer, and acceptance.* Each, I believe, attends to the spiritual wound common to resentments. One strategy may be preferable to another in a given situation, more than one may be useful in another.

Common to all resentments is the experience of having been betrayed, wronged, "had," taken advantage of, or violated. An injustice has been done –and you've come out on the short end. The situation demands righting; the rightful order of things must be restored. But how?

Let's rule out two options from the start: getting drunk and physical violence. A belt, whether of John Barleycorn or from the fist, will only make matters worse. And parading your grievance in front of others, as human this may be, also provides little more than temporary numbing of the sting of your wound. (Having your friends concur that you've been "screwed" only fuels the indignation; it does not unscrew the resentment!)

(1) **Prayer** - The Big Book suggests prayer; specifically, praying to show those who wronged us "the same tolerance, pity, and patience that we would cheerfully grant a sick friend" (67, top). Praying for the person or thing(s) one resents is also suggested in Wynn L's story, "Freedom From Bondage," in the second, third and fourth editions.

(2) **Assertiveness** - The assertive strategy involves confronting – in an assertive, *not* aggressive, fashion – your wrongdoer over the damage or harm done. All things considered, this is usually the most helpful or satisfying method, as it allows for a face-to-face airing of the grievance. (The strategy can be effective even if your wrongdoer remains deaf to your overtures. Just guard against arguing the point, or buying into any denial or attempt to shift the focus of the wrongdoing onto you.)

This approach is counter-indicted in situations where you either know or have reason to believe that additional harm may come your way by confronting the one who has wronged. The reality is, not everyone is blessed with an inner eye, or receptive to looking at their wrongdoing or role in a conflict. Insisting on an apology or acknowledgment of the harm done by such a person may exacerbate the situation, or keep you mired in your resentment. Remember: The wrong does *not* have to be acknowledged by the other party or parties for you to heal. (A variation on the assertive strategy is to write a letter to your wrongdoer. Or perhaps two letters: one that consigns the person to Hades, the other edited to mail.)

(3) **Acceptance** – Ownership of one's wound *without* any censoring or censuring of oneself. In this regard, acceptance entails an allowance for one's humanity and humanness; an understanding that we are all subject to the vagaries and vicissitudes of life. Acceptance does *not* mean that you forgive the one who has hurt or wronged you; that you now trust that individual; or that you are, or will ever be, ready or willing to break bread with them. Acceptance is first and foremost about healing and moving on from the wrong, *not* resuming a relationship with the wrongdoer. Acceptance is also *not intellectualizing*. It *rarely* comes about overnight, or in the time it takes to read the paragraph beginning, "And acceptance is the answer to *all* my problems today. . ." in Dr. Paul O's story, "Doctor, Alcoholic, Addict" (renamed "Acceptance Was The Answer" for the fourth edition). Nor should acceptance be understood as the absence of feelings about the wrong (if anything, it is an allowance for and openness to one's feelings); or a lasting state of mind, i.e., one may have to work at returning to a state of acceptance just as one may have to work at returning to an admission of step one.

Bottom line: In the presence of resentment, act, don't react; act out of what is in the best interest of your healing and spiritual wellbeing, don't react out of your story or the wrong done to you.

☞ The Big Book makes no mention of anger or resentment toward oneself, though these too make for spiritual illness and seem equally deserved of inclusion on page 65's template. It is important to allow for error and mistake making, for self-inventory without self-condemnation, and for not always acting or responding to a situation *perfectly* or in the manner of the idealized self.

Page 67

Top. "We asked God to help us show them the same tolerance, pity, and patience that we would cheerfully grant a sick friend." Prayer as suggested spiritual antidote to resentments. Strategy spelled out in Wynn L.'s story, "Freedom From Bondage" (Third edition, 551-553; Fourth edition, 551-552).

Top. "When a person offended we said to ourselves, 'This is a sick [person]. How can I be helpful to him [or her]? God save me from being angry. Thy will be done.'" Detaching from (not personalizing or assuming responsibility for) someone else's selfish or inconsiderate ways often helps take much of the sting out of their behavior. You're undoubtedly not the first person they've hurt or rolled over, and not likely to be the last. To regard their conduct as a reflection on you only rubs shame into an existing injury. (This notion of detachment may be compared to gazing at monkeys in a zoo. You observe them doing all sorts of things monkeys do – swing from the fake tree with hanging rubber tire, eat, sleep, groom one another, and attend to nature's call – all without considering any of it as having anything to do with you. Of course, if one of the monkeys should toss a banana in your direction, you might want to step aside or duck. It's unlikely, however, that you'd regard such monkey business as an assault on your very being. Or sufficient cause to want the poor creature taken out and shot. So, the next time someone lets a door close in your face, or your served attitude along with that overly-priced latte, just remember: "Monkeys in a cage!")

☞ *Important cautionary word:* This does *not* mean that we never confront or assert ourselves with one who offends, or seek out assistance in conflict resolution, or remove ourselves from an unhealthy or abusive relationship or situation.

☞ It's one thing to get angry and quite another to stay stuck in one's anger, one thing to be angry and quite another to act out in an aggressive or destructive fashion. Anger is a feeling, a natural human response to being slighted or wronged, and asking your Higher Power to save you from getting angry may be as futile and nonsensical as asking your Higher Power to save you from laughing at a wonderful joke.

Mid. "Referring to our list again. Putting out of our minds the wrongs others had done, we resolutely looked for our own mistakes." Spiritual growth here centering on the following: first, a fearless and searching inventory of how we have "placed ourselves in a position to be hurt" (our own role in conflicts or discord); second, admitting to our faults or mistakes; and third, making restitution for harm done.

☞ *Notable exception:* There are, of course, situations in which one is *truly innocent* of another's wrongdoing, where there is *no* basis for a self-survey of "our own mistakes." I am thinking in particular of childhood abuse, neglect, or abandonment, though these are by no means the only instances in which one may be the victim of unprovoked harm. While rage and resentments associated with such wounds still beg for resolution, especially for those seeking a spiritual remedy for an alcohol problem, the only "mistake" here, if you will, is that of simply *being,* or *being in the wrong place at the wrong time.* (The guidance and support of a therapist well versed in trauma resolution may be of vital importance in such situations.)

Bot. "When we saw our faults we listed them. We placed them before us in black and white." An additional column may be added to the template on page 63:

I'm Resentful At	The Cause	Affects My	My Faults

Bot. "This short word [fear] somehow touches about every aspect of our lives. It was an evil and corroding thread . . . It set in motion trains of circumstances which brought us misfortune we felt we didn't deserve." Self-centered fear – the fear of losing what we have, the fear not getting what we want – as the chief activator of our defects is commented upon by Bill W. in the *12x12,* page 76.

Page 68
Top. "We reviewed our fears thoroughly. We put them on paper. . ." This format is taken from *A Program for You* (Copyright 1991 by Hazelden Foundation. Reprinted by permission of Hazelden Foundation; 115):

I'm Afraid Of	The Cause	Affects My*

* Affects one or more of the following: self-esteem, pride, personal relationships, material security, emotional security, acceptable sexual relations, hidden sexual relations, ambitions. (115)

Top. ". . . why we had them. Wasn't it because self-reliance failed us." Step One: We admitted we were licked, that self-sufficiency was not sufficient. For example, we couldn't trust or rely on it to keep us sober.

Mid. "Just to the extent that we do as we think He would have us, and humbly rely on Him, does He enable us to match calamity with serenity." (Or, just to the extent that we do as we think AA would have us, and humbly rely on it, does it enable us to navigate our way through difficult times without drinking.) From the top of page 63:

> When we sincerely took such a position, all sorts of remarkable things followed. We had a new Employer. Being all powerful, He provided what we needed, if we kept close to Him and performed His work well. . .As we felt new power flow in, as we enjoyed peace of mind, as we discovered we could face life successfully, as we became conscious of His presence, we began to lose our *fear* of today, tomorrow or the hereafter. We were reborn. (63) (Italics added.)

Mid. "We never apologize to anyone for depending upon our Creator." Or for being a member of Alcoholics Anonymous.

Bot. "We ask Him to remove our fear. . ." See again Third Step Prayer on page 63, and Seventh Step Prayer on 76.

Page 69
Bot. "We must be willing to make amends where we have done harm, provided that we do not bring about still more harm in so doing." See step nine: "Made direct amends to such people wherever possible, *except when to do so would injure them or others.*" (Italics added.)

Bot. "In meditation, we ask God what we should do about each specific matter." Step eleven (see page 86, bottom, and 87, bottom).

Page 70
Mid. "To sum up about sex: We earnestly pray for the right idea, for guidance in each questionable situation, for sanity, and for the strength to do the right thing." For some sage words regarding "'boy meets girl on A.A. campus [or treatment],' and love follows at first sight," the reader is referred to the *12x12*, page 119.

Bot. "If we have been thorough about our personal inventory, we have written down a lot." While Chapter 5 spotlights resentments, fear, and sex conduct as grist for the fourth step mill, self-survey is by no means limited to these potential roadblocks. Thus, from Earl T's story, "He Sold Himself Short":

> Dr. Bob led me through all these steps. At the moral inventory, he brought up several of my bad personality traits or character defects, such as selfishness, conceit, jealousy, carelessness, intolerance, ill-temper, sarcasm, and resentments. (Second edition, 292).

And a survey of the Seven Deadly Sins (pride, sloth, gluttony, greed, lust, envy and anger) is offered in the *12x12* (48) as an appropriate starting point for a little soul-surgery (to borrow a phrase from the Oxford Group).

☞ As the scope of step four is variable, so also is the time frame. For instance, a person's step four focus might be on avoidant behavior during her initial three months in recovery; while another individual might reflect on the headway he's made in untangling himself from an unhealthy family dynamic since his previous inventory.

☞ The oft-floated idea that step four need be worked only once; that a regular and rigorous working of step ten is thereafter sufficient to keep the spiritual traveler on the Road of Happy Destiny, would seem to overlook the value that evolving perspective has accurate self-appraisal.

Page 71

Top. "We hope you are convinced that God can remove whatever self-will has blocked you off from Him." Expression of grace. God can remove whatever blocks you off from God. And, observes Linda Mercadante: "God *wants* to free us. God's grace will not let us rest in our inertia and complacency . . . Grace surrounds us, and if we open ourselves to this offer and relationship, we come home." (*VS, 170*)

☞ In a similar fashion, AA can help the alcoholic recover, and AA *wants* to help the alcoholic recover: "Each group has but one primary purpose—to carry its message to the alcoholic who still suffers" (Tradition Five). Statement of purpose is also reflected in AA's Preamble.

☞ Recurrent Big Book theme: The reader is challenged to identify what needs changing in her *own* backyard, then pointed outside of self for help in changing what she finds.

Top. "If you have already made a decision, and an inventory of your grosser handicaps. . ." Steps three and four.

☞ Chapter 5's focus on dishonesty, self-centeredness, resentment, and fear as the most objectionable or egregious manifestations of self is reflective of AA's Oxford Group roots. (*OOGA*, 88-89, 303). For a good read on the Oxford Group and its influence on AA, see *The Oxford Group & Alcoholics Anonymous,* by Dick B.

Chapter 6

Into Action

Summary - Provides rationale for working step five ("The best reason first: If we skip this vital step, we may not overcome drinking."), and an overview of steps six to eleven. A statement of the Twelve Promises is also found in the chapter (83, bottom, to 84).

Page 72
Top. "We have been trying to get a new attitude, a new relationship with our Creator. . ." Higher Power relationship – *connection* – as shield against the first drink. See again the last paragraph, page 43: "The alcoholic at certain times has no effective mental defense against the first drink . . .His defense must come from a Higher Power"; and last of the three pertinent ideas on page 60: "(c) That God could and would [lift our destructive obsession with alcohol] *if He were sought."* (Italics added.)

". . . and to discover the obstacles in our path. *Whatever* stands between the alcoholic and his or her Higher Power (or AA program, fellowship, sponsor, etc.)

☞ The word *obstacle* strikes me as more user-friendly than either shortcoming or defect of character, and for this reason may be of greater use by folks who wrestle with excessive shame or inaccurate self-perception.

Too, *obstacle* casts a wider net than either shortcoming or defect, which seem more at home with manifestations of egregious pride or self-will than other potential impediments to relationship building, i.e., abuse, abandonment or neglect, chronic pain and mental health illness, and warfare, oppression or other phenomenon that can traumatize the soul. I believe this is in keeping with Mercadante when she notes:

> 'Self-will run riot' is by far not the only way to turn from God. In our day it may be the less common way. Identifying the core human problem as inordinate self-will or pride obscures crucial distinctions. It can reinforce and even inadvertently praise the "sin of self-loss." It can fail to identify actual coercion, *han*, and victimization. When one's core problem is truly a turning from God, a disorientation from our proper source, this can come about through inordinate self-loss as much as through inordinate self-will." (*VS*, 39)

Bot. "Time after time newcomers have tried to keep to themselves certain facts about their lives. Trying to avoid this humbling experience, they have turned to easier methods. Almost invariably they got drunk." Related words are found on the bottom of page 56 to the top of 57 in the *12x12,* and these lines from Chapter 2, page 25 of the text:

Almost none of us liked the self-searching, the leveling of our pride, the confession of shortcomings which the process requires for its successful consummation. But we saw that it really worked in others, and we had come to believe in the hopelessness and futility of life as we had been living it.

☞ Additional benefits of working step five include: freedom from loneliness and isolation; lessening of false pride and shame; a sense of communion and shared humanity; self-forgiveness and humility; closeness to one's Creator; and direction for continued emotional and spiritual growth. Similar gains are noted in this citation from Marty Mann's story, "Women Suffer Too":

> Talking things over with them, great floods of enlightenment showed me myself as I really was – and I was like them. We all had hundreds of character traits, fears and phobias, likes and dislikes, in common. Suddenly I could accept myself, faults and all, as I was – for weren't we all like that? And, accepting, I felt a new inner comfort and the willingness and strength to do something about the traits I couldn't live with. (Second edition, 229)

Page 73
Mid. "More than most people, the alcoholic leads a double life." Thus from "Me An Alcoholic?":

> When I try to reconstruct what my life was like "before," I see a coin with two faces.
>
> One, the side I turned to myself and the world, was respectable – even, in some ways, distinguished . . .
>
> The other side of the coin was sinister, baffling. I was inwardly unhappy most of the time. There would be times when the life of respectability and achievement seemed insufferably dull – I had to break out. This I would do by going completely "bohemian" for a night, getting drunk, and rolling home with the dawn. Next day, remorse would be on me like a tiger. I'd claw my way back to respectability and stay there – until the inevitable next time. (Second edition, 419)

Page 75
Mid. "Once we have taken this step, withholding nothing, we are delighted." I think it important for folks to watch their expectations when approaching step five. Self-survey, especially in the presence of another, is rarely easy; and it seems just as likely for a piece of soul surgery to end in pain and fatigue as in wonder and awe. Bottom line: I suspect there are as many different fifth step experiences as there are instances of people working the step. It seems a good idea to allow yourself to be wherever your fifth step

work takes you – rather than entering the process with some pre-conceived idea of being "rocketed into the fourth dimension."

Page 76

Top. "If we can answer to our satisfaction, we then look at *Step Six*." ("We're entirely ready to have God remove all these defects of character.") The reader is cautioned against being scared off by the words *entirely ready*. As Bill noted in the *12x12*, "practically nobody" has this sense of readiness; the best one can do is to reach for it. (65-66, top) Thus step six might be understood: "We [aimed to become] entirely ready to have God remove all these defects of character."

☞ Implicit in seeking help in removing obstacles is a willingness to *surrender them;* a willingness to cease indulging or enjoying them, or seeking cover behind them.

Top. "When ready, we something like this . . ." Step Seven: "Humbly asked Him to remove our shortcomings." As the alcoholic is unable to remain abstinent on the basis of self-will or self-knowledge, so too she is unable to change (remove her impediments to spiritual growth) solely on the basis of self-will or self-knowledge.

☞ Character building or obstacle removal may also be aided by reaching out to one's sponsor, counselor, therapist, AA group, etc. For example, reaching out to one's peers in treatment for assistance in resentment resolution is a demonstration of working step seven (and by implication, six as well).

☞ Meaningful change *cannot* be manufactured or summoned on command. Nor is it likely to bloom from a solitary effort or a one-time appeal for help. Demanding that God, or anyone, fix you or fix you on your timetable probably won't work. Remember: It's *humbling asking*. As a sponsor might observe to his pigeon: "In step three you turned your will and your life over to the care of God. So it is now God's business – *not* yours – when change occurs, i.e., you bring the effort, God brings the results."

It is also important to guard against unrealistic expectations around the *removal* of one's spiritual pests. For most of these, gradual improvement – *not* total elimination – is the norm (*12x12*, 65); i.e., reducing mountains to molehills, or transforming beasts into periodic pests. Expecting all of one's defects or obstacles to be gone by the time one leaves treatment, or has a year in recovery, or some other arbitrary benchmark is a sure setup for disappointment (and again, an instance of trying to control!).

☞ Note the similarity between the Seventh and Third Step Prayers (63). Both speak of surrender, service to others, and performing God's will. Too, the theme of steps one, two and three ("I can't. You can. Help me.) is simply repeated in five to seve, with the focus of the initial three steps on the merciless obsession, and that of steps five, six and seven on the problem of self.

☞ I fear that short shrift is often made of steps six and seven (the Big Book itself devotes but two small paragraphs to them). They are, however, vital to the alcoholic's spiritual growth and the next logical directives (or spiritual exercises) after four and five. That is, in step four the alcoholic inventories his obstacles to serenity and sobriety, and in step five he admits to them. The next question seems to be, "So what are you going to do about these pests?" If the response is a variation on little to nothing, the alcoholic ought not be surprised if the quality of his life remains unchanged, or he finds himself back with the bottle. He hasn't done anything to make his life better or to escape the long arm of King Alcohol. (Patients in Hazelden's long-term residential program often wondered, "What's going to be different this time? My standard reply, "Whatever *you* make different.")

Mid. "Now we need more action, without which we find that 'Faith without works is dead." Or believing in the AA program, without working the AA program, spells relapse!

Mid. "We have a list of all persons we had harmed and to whom we are willing to make amends. We made it when we took inventory." Step four.

☞ It is likely that the alcoholic's step eight list will continue to expand, especially in the infancy of recovery. It's a sign of spiritual growth. As she loses her self-centered focus, as her denial abates, as she becomes ever more aware of how her words and behavior and bottles impacted others, additional names are sure to line up for inclusion.

Mid. "We attempt to sweep away the debris which has accumulated out of our effort to live on self-will and run the show ourselves." Again, the spiritual dimension of alcoholism – the problem of self – as "the root of our troubles." (62)

Bot. "Remember it was agreed at the beginning *we would go to any lengths for victory over alcohol.*" Again from page 58: "If you want what we have and are willing to go to any length to get it – then you are ready to take certain steps."

Page 77
Mid. "But our man is sure to be impressed with a sincere desire to set right the wrong. He is going to be more interested in a demonstration of good will than in our talk of spiritual discoveries." A similar idea is expressed on page 83: "Our behavior will convince them more than our words. We must remember that ten or twenty years of drunkenness would make a skeptic out of anyone."

Page 78
Top. "It should not matter, however, if someone does throw us out of his office. We have made our demonstration, done our part. It's water over the damn." It's good to remember step one when working step nine: you have say over your amends, not over how others respond to them.

Mid. "Most alcoholics owe money. We do not dodge our creditors . . . Nor are we afraid of disclosing our alcoholism on the theory it may cause financial harm." His resistance to out himself with friends and creditors about his drinking was a factor in Dr. Bob's relapse shortly after his initial meeting with Bill W. (*PIO,* 149, 155-156) "Why, he argued, should he lose the remainder of his business, only to bring still more suffering to is family by foolishly admitting his plight to people from whom he made his livelihood? He would do anything, he said, but that." (155). Again from Chapter 5: "At some of these we balked. We thought we could find an easier, softer way. But we could not." (58)

Page 79
Top. ". . . we ask that we be given strength and direction to do the right thing. . ." Step Eleven.

Top. "We may lose our position or reputation or face jail, but we are willing. We have to be. We must not shrink at anything." An important caveat to this rigorous and rigid working of step nine: ". . . except when to do so would injure them or others." Hence the paragraph (and pages) immediately following: "Usually, however, other people are involved. Therefore, we are not to be the hasty and foolish martyr who would needlessly sacrifice others to save himself from the alcoholic pit."

☞ Problematic cases are sure to present themselves. Still, the gravest loss from most amends is that of face or false pride – *not* family, finances, or freedom. Thorney situations should not be used to excuse the readily doable step nines.

Page 80
Bot. "He saw that he had to place the outcome in God's hands or he would soon start drinking again . . ." Step three.

Page 81
Bot. "We are sorry for what we have done [adultery] and, God willing, it shall not be repeated." I don't reckon it a good idea to put the responsibility for fidelity squarely on the shoulders of one's Higher Power.

Page 82
Bot. "The alcoholic is a tornado roaring his way through the lives of others." Self-will run riot. Evident whether the alcoholic is dry or well-fortified. (Alcoholics, of course, do not have the market on self-centeredness or living by self-propulsion.)

Bot. "Hearts are broken. Sweet relations are dead." Alcohol-related unmanageability. See also page 18, top: "An illness of this sort – and we have come to believe it an illness – involves those about us in a way no other human sickness can."

Page 83

Top. "Yes, there is a long period of reconstruction ahead." Amends making – working to change for the better our relations with others – as *process*, not event.

Top. "Their defects may be glaring, but the chances are that our own actions are partly responsible." See the *12x12*, page 78, mid paragraph.

Mid. "There may be some wrongs we cannot fully right." Even here, however, working to change one's behavior so as to minimize a repeat of these wrongs is a form of amends-making.

Bot. "If we are painstaking about this phase of our development, we will be amazed before we are halfway through." The Twelve Promises. A suggested format for considering whether the promises are being realized is to change each from a declarative statement into a question in the first person. For instance, "We are going to know a new freedom and a new happiness," might become, "Am I beginning to know a new freedom from my preoccupation with drinking?" And, "We will not regret the past nor wish to shut the door on it," becomes, "Am I beginning to make peace with my story, beginning to embrace it rather than avoid it, beginning to talk about my drinking and drug use and its impact on others?"

☞ I'm not sure why the Promises appear between steps nine and ten. I'm doubtful, however, that the book's authors had an exact time frame in mind for their occurrence. That "they are being fulfilled amongst us – sometimes quickly, sometimes slowly" (84) certainly suggests the need to be flexible in this matter. Too, these are certainly not the only promises or inscriptions of hope in the text. The Big Book is generously sprinkled with them, beginning with the title page itself:

ALCOHOLICS ANONYMOUS
The Story of
How Many Thousands of Men and Women
Have Recovered from Alcoholism

Then we have: "The tremendous fact for every one of us is that we have discovered a common solution. We have a way out . . .This is the great news this book carries to those who suffer from alcoholism." (17) Now there's a message of hope to hang a hangover on!

Additional promises are certainly noted on page 25 (*"There is a solution . . . The great fact is just this, and nothing less: That we have had deep and effective spiritual experiences which have revolutionized our whole attitude towards life, toward our fellows and towards God's universe. . ."*); and page 75 ("Once we have taken this step [five], withholding nothing, we are delighted. . .The feeling that the drink problem has disappeared will often come strongly. We feel we are on the Broad Highway, walking hand in hand with the Spirit of the Universe."). And what about the popular opening to Chapter 5: "Rarely have we seen a person fail who has thoroughly followed our path." Certainly, the stuff that dreams are made of. Or these lines from 163: "You forget that you have just tapped a source of power much greater than yourself. To duplicate, with such backing, what we have accomplished is only a matter of willingness, patience and labor." And last, from the text's final page: "See to it that your relationship with Him is right, and great events will come to pass for you and countless others. This is the Great Fact for us." In the end, the presentation and timing of these spiritual desserts seem of less significance than the promise that they will occur – "if we work for them." (84)

☞ On the other hand, speculation is certainly fun. So the one thought I do have as to why the Promises (or at least those cited on pages 83-84) may be sandwiched between steps nine and ten is that Dr. Bob's first day of continuous sobriety (and AA's birthday, June 10, 1935) is marked by his decision to begin the work of amends-making:

> He saw that he would have to face his problems squarely that God might give him mastery. One morning he took the bull by the horns and set out to tell those he feared what his trouble had been . . . He trembled as he went about, for this might mean ruin, particularly to a person in his line of business. At midnight he came home exhausted, but very happy. He had not had a drink since. (156)

Page 84
Top. The final promise in the first paragraph ("We will suddenly realize that God is doing for us what we could not do for ourselves") is step two ("Came to believe that a power greater than ourselves could restore us to sanity.") is the last of the three pertinent ideas on page 60 ("That God could and would if He were sought.").

Mid. "They [the Promises] will always materialize if we work for them." Yet another promise! Some identify this as the last or Twelfth Promise itself. (*PS,* 12)

Mid. "Our next function is to grow in understanding and effectiveness." Step ten as *a growth – not* maintenance – step. It is impossible to continue one's spiritual housekeeping and not grow.

Bot. "Continue to watch for selfishness, dishonesty, resentment and fear." Premium placed on standing guard over these spiritual pests reflect AA's roots in the Oxford Group, where they were regarded as "the most common and objectionable manifestations of self that needed to be eliminated." (*OOGA,* 303) These are not, of course, the only impediments to living in relationship with one's Higher Power. Each alcoholic has his or her own constellation or assortment. They come with *being human.*

☞ Implicit in Step Ten is recognition of our essential finiteness, not as alcoholics, but as human beings. Mistakes, wrongs and wrongdoing come with the territory. Indeed, step ten exits to help net the endless drippings of our humanity.

Bot. "When these crop up we ask God at once to remove them." Steps six and seven.

Bot. "We discuss them with someone immediately. . ." Step five.

". . .and make amends quickly if we have harmed anyone." Steps eight and nine.

Bot. "Then we resolutely turn our thoughts to someone we can help." Step twelve.

☞ Step ten does not say that we are *always* wrong! As Bill himself observes in the 12x12, self-survey is not always done in red-ink. (93) For readers inclined to overlook good efforts and deeds, I'd suggest tacking the following phrase onto number ten: *and when we were right, promptly accepted it!*

Bot. "And we have ceased fighting anything or anyone – including alcohol." Surrender. Both a letting go of trying to play God or "run the whole show," *and* a turning to God for direction in playing one's role in the show. Self in need of redirection is also noted on page 103, bottom: "*After all, our problems were of our own making. Bottles were only a symbol. Besides, we have stopped fighting anybody or anything. We have to!*"

Bot. "For by this time sanity will have returned." A lifting of the alcoholic obsession (with intoxication or controlled use) through the intervening grace of one's Higher Power.

Bot. "If tempted, we recall from it as we would from a hot flame." Contrast with pre-liberation days on page 24:

> The almost certain consequences that follow taking even a glass of beer do not crowd into the mind to deter us. If these thoughts occur, they are hazy and readily supplanted by the old threadbare idea that this time we shall handle ourselves like other people [alcoholic obsession]. There is a complete failure of the kind of defense that keeps one from putting his hand on a hot stove.

Page 85.
Top. "We feel as though we had been placed in a position of neutrality – safe and protected." The experience of being in a safe spiritual harbor (12x12, 35) is frequently had at AA.

Top. ". . .the problem has been removed." Again, the lifting of the alcoholic obsession.

Mid. ". . . so long as we keep in fit spiritual condition." That is, so long as one keeps spiritual sludge (dishonesty, self-centeredness, resentment, fear, etc.) from clogging the channel to her Higher Power.

Mid. "It is easy to let up on the spiritual program of action and rest on our laurels. We are headed for trouble if we do, for alcohol is a subtle foe." Complacency as a foe of recovery. Cautionary word repeated in these lines from "The Keys Of The Kingdom":

> A.A. is not a plan for recovery that can be finished and done with. It is a way of life . . . Keeping one foot in front of the other is essential for maintaining our arrestment. Others may idle in a retrogressive groove without too much danger, but retrogression can spell death for us. (Second edition, 311)

Mid. "We are not cured of alcoholism. What we really have is a daily reprieve contingent on the maintenance of our spiritual condition." The obsession lifted, the illness in remission, the alcoholic "placed in a position of neutrality – "safe and protected" – all contingent on the maintenance of his or her Higher Power relationship.

Mid. "Every day is a day when we must carry the vision of God's will into all of our activities." Remember step Twelve: ". . . and to practice these principles in all our affairs."

Mid. "'How can I serve thee – Thy will (not mine) be done.' These are thoughts which must go with us constantly. We can exercise our will power along this line all we wish. It is the proper use of the will." See the *12x12,* page 40, last paragraph.

Bot. "If we have carefully followed directions. . ." The Twelve Steps as directions.

". . .we have begun to sense the flow of His Spirit into us. From "Bill's Story": "My friend promised when these things were done [worked various Oxford Group tenets] I would enter upon a new relationship with my Creator; that I would have the elements of a way of living which answered all my problems." (13)

Bot. "To some extent we have become God-conscious." Identified with spiritual awakening in Appendix II: "Most of us think this awareness of a Power greater than ourselves is the essence of spiritual experiences. Our more religious members call it 'God-consciousness.'"

Bot. "*Step Eleven* suggests prayer and meditation." Seeking to improve one's conscious contact – one's relationship – through consultation and communion with some Power greater than self. Morning devotion and quiet time were considered "musts" by early member of the still un-named fellowship (*DB;* 131, 136).

☞ In working step three the alcoholic turns her will and her life over to the care and direction of her God; and in working step eleven she seeks to know and follow God's will for her. Alternatively, in step three the alcoholic lets go of his own ideas about his drinking problem in favor of those suggested by AA (*12x12*, 35); and in step eleven he seeks to know and do as AA (sponsor, steps, fellowship) prescribes for the management of his illness.

☞ How might the atheist work step eleven? How to seek conscious contact with what *is not?* Perhaps by devoting oneself to seeking connection with what *is:* the blimps on the "radar" we choose to ignore; the needs and challenges that beg for our attention; and the unfinished business that won't resolve itself – that is there with us as we lay our head on the pillow at night, and greets us as we rub the sleepy bugs from our eyes in the morn. To allow these matters into our field of vision, to integrate these truths and matters into our daily doings seems indeed the stuff and challenge of step eleven.

Page 86
Top. "When we retire at night, we constructively review our day." Step Ten – specifically, a day's end inventory.

Top. "Have we kept something to ourselves which should be discussed with another person at once?" Dishonesty through omission; for example, wanting to drink!

Mid. "On awakening let us think about the twenty-four hours ahead." Thus from Dick S's story, "He Had To Be Shown":

> The very simple program they advised me to follow was that I should ask to know God's will for me for that one day, and then, to the best of my ability, to follow that, and at night to express my gratefulness to God for the things that had happened to me during the day. When I left the hospital I tried this for a day and it worked, for a week and it worked, and for a month, and it worked—and then for a year and it still worked. It has continued to work now for nearly eighteen years." (Second edition, 208-09)

Bot. "Here we ask God for inspiration, an intuitive thought or a decision. . . We are often surprised how the right answers come after we have tried this for a while." A cautionary word about bringing one's problems *exclusively* to one's Higher Power is offered in the *12x12*, pages 103-04.

Page 87
Top. "We usually conclude this period of meditation with a prayer that we be shown all through the day what our next step is to be, that we be given whatever we need to take care of such problems." The spiritual thrust of the "Eleventh Step Prayer" is given expression in the above citation from Dick S's story.

Mid. "We are careful never to pray for our own selfish ends." For example, "Lord, get me out of this DWI and I'll never drink again!" Or, "Dear God, please let me win the lottery." Contrast the self-serving nature of these entreaties with the Third and Seventh Steps Prayers on pages 63 and 76, respectively.

Mid. "If we belong to a religious denomination which requires a definite morning devotion, we attend to that also." Again, early AAs stressed the importance of "quiet time" or "morning devotion" for recovery. Indeed, such practices were accorded greater importance than meeting attendance, which was initially regarded as "desirable," not vital. (*DB*, 131, 136)

☞ The slogan, "Don't drink. Go to meetings. And read the Big Book" is *not* in the Big Book! The Fellowship's framers were of the notion that the text alone was sufficient to start the newcomer on the road to recovery:

> "The early expectation was that drunks would order the book, make surrender, and as they got back to their jobs and lives would help other drunks. Once in a while, those who had new candidates might gather so the newcomers could ask questions and meet other alkies. The fact that it did not work out that way was more slowly accepted by Bill [W.] than by most others." (*VS, 12-13*)

This early expectation is implicit in the Foreword To First Edition: "We shall be interested to hear from those who are getting results from this book, particularly from those who have commenced to work with other alcoholics" (xiv), and also Chapter 11, "A Vision For You": "Thus we grow. And so can you, though you be but one man with this book in your hand. We believe and hope it contains all you will need to begin." (163)

Page 88
Top. "We are then in much less danger of excitement, fear, anger, worry, self-pity, or foolish decisions." Abstinence-based unmanageability as consequence of living by self-propulsion, or trying to run the whole show (60-62).

Top. "We do not tire so easily, for we are not burning up energy foolishly as we did when we were trying to arrange life to suit ourselves." See again discussion of "The Actor" on pages 60-62.

Top. "We alcoholics are undisciplined." Self-will.

Top. "So we let God discipline us in the simple way we have just outlined." Step eleven.

Top. "The next chapter is entirely devoted to *Step Twelve.*" Actually, only the second part of step twelve: "Having had a spiritual awakening as the result of these steps, *we tried to carry this message to alcoholics,* and to practice these principles in all our affairs." (Italics added.)

Chapter 7

Working With Others

Summary - Majority of the chapter is devoted to carrying the message ("the foundation stone of your recovery") to the still suffering alcoholic, as well as offering help and "your way of life to family members." Rule also suggested about being in "a place where there is drinking." The text's recommended strategies for working with others (education on illness model of alcoholism; not imposing diagnosis on the alcoholic; cautionary word about enabling or other dynamics that may undermine efforts at recovery; family assistance, and acceptance of one's powerlessness over the problem drinker) are integral features of twelve-step based recovery centers today.

Top. "Practical experience shows that nothing will so much insure immunity from drinking as intensive work with other alcoholics." Bill W's own "immunity" through twelve step work is cited in Chapter 1:

> I was not too well at the time, and was plagued by waves of self-pity and resentment. This sometimes nearly drove me back to drink, but I soon found that when all other measures failed, work with another alcoholic would save the day. Many times, I have gone to my old hospital in despair. On talking to a man there, I would be amazingly lifted up and set on my feet. It is a design for living that works in rough going. (15)

☞ Rationale and reward for twelve step work are also cited by Dr. Bob in "Dr. Bob's Nightmare" (Second edition, 180-81):

> I spend a great deal of time passing on what I learned to others who want and need it badly. I do it for four reasons:
>
> 1. Sense of duty.
> 2. It is a pleasure.
> 3. Because in so doing I am paying my debt to the man who took time to pass it on to me.
> 4. Because every time I do it I take out a little more insurance for myself against a possible slip.

Page 90
Top. "If he does not want to stop drinking, don't waste time trying to persuade him." Permission to detach, echoed in these lines on page 96: "We find it a waste of time to keep chasing a man who cannot or will not work with you. If you leave such a person alone, he may soon become convinced that he cannot recover by himself."

Page 90
Bot. "But say nothing, for the moment, of how that was accomplished." Prospect may be scared off by talk of God or matters spiritual.

Mid. ". . .the queer mental condition surrounding the first drink. . ." The obsession of the mind.

Mid. "And be careful not to brand him an alcoholic. Let him draw his own conclusion." Acceptance must come from within.

Page 93
Top. "He can choose any conception he likes, provided it makes sense to him." Thus Ebby's suggestion to Bill: "Why don't you choose your own conception of God." (12)

Top. *The main thing is that he be willing to believe in a Power greater than himself and that he live by spiritual principles.* Text is written in the spirit of accommodation. See also the method of substitution (making AA itself one's higher power) in the *12x12,* page 27.

Page 95
Top. "You will be more successful with alcoholics if you do not exhibit any passion for crusade or reform. Never talk down to an alcoholic from any moral or spiritual hilltop; simply lay out the kit of spiritual tools for his inspection." A hard lesson learned by Bill during his early efforts at carrying the message: after six months of teaching and preaching to scores of men, no one had sobered up! (*PIO,* 132) Dejected, Bill called on his friend Dr. Silkworth, who suggested that Bill had been putting the cart before the horse – the spiritual before the medical – scaring off prospects in the process. Instead of preaching about God, advised Silkworth, Bill first needed to focus the alcoholic's attention on the double-edged sword dangling above his head: the obsession that condemned the man to drink, and the allergy that insured self-destruction. (*12x12,* 22) Only then, only after his man understood the gravity of his situation, should Bill introduce the idea of moral psychology as a means of healing. (*PIO,* 133)

Bot. "If he thinks he can do the job in some other way, or prefers some other spiritual approach, encourage him to follow his conscience." Again, AA does not represent itself as the *only* way out of King Alcohol's mad realm. It simply shines a light on *the* way taken by its earliest members. (See again Foreword to Second Edition, xxi).

Page 96
Top. "Do not be discouraged if your prospect does not respond at once. Search out another alcoholic and try again." Remember the words: ". . .we *tried* to carry this message to alcoholics . . ." (italics added). Not every twelfth step call is a "success." Too, sown seeds often need to be watered with a few more drinks before they bear fruit (Bill required additional "lubrication" before taking Ebby's words to heart.)

Bot. "Be certain . . .that he is not trying to impose on you for money, connections, or shelter. Permit that and you only harm him." Don't enable.

Page 97
Top. "Never avoid these responsibilities, but be sure you are doing the right thing if you assume them. Helping others is the foundation stone of your recovery." Chapter 7 speaks of twelve step work exclusively in terms of carrying the message to new recruits. Additional examples of this vital work are noted in the *12x12,* page 110, bottom.

Bot. "The family should be offered your way of life." Al-Anon was founded in 1951.

Bot. "Should they accept and practice spiritual principles, there is a much better chance that the head of the family will recover." While a change in family dynamics may well necessitate a change in the alcoholic's routine, there is no guarantee that recovery will ensue. Still, "the family will find life more bearable." (97)

Page 100
Top. "Follow the dictates of a Higher Power . . ." Step Eleven.

". . . and you will presently live in a new and wonderful world, no matter what your present circumstances!" Another promise.

Bot. "Assuming we are spiritually fit . . ." Assuming the channel to one's Higher Power is not blocked by spiritual sludge, assuming one is living in relationship with one's Higher Power.

Page 101
Top. "An alcoholic who cannot meet them, still has an alcoholic mind; there is something the matter with his spiritual status." An important caveat: *Everyone* has vulnerable moments – especially in the infancy of recovery. At such times, I think it not only prudent to keep out of slippery situations but also a sign of humility and spiritual maturity; that is, acceptance of one's vulnerability and limitations.

Page 102
Bot. "Many of us keep liquor in our homes. We often need it to carry green recruits through a severe hangover." Remember that the Big Book was published in 1939 when treatment and detoxification facilities were few. Issues of health, safety, and liability certainly rule against such practices today.

Page 103
Mid. *"After all, our problems were of our own making. Bottles were only a symbol."* Again, as the text unfolds, the spiritual dimension of the illness receives star billing. Bottles emerge as both symbol and symptom of living

out of orientation with one's Higher Power (or relapse emerges as the result of *falling out* of relationship with AA program and fellowship).

Chapter 8

To Wives

Summary - A Twelve Step call by wives of alcoholics on wives of alcoholics.

Page 104

Mid. "We want the wives of Alcoholics Anonymous to address the wives of men who drink too much." In reality, Bill himself wrote the chapter. As Lois observed years later to Francis Hartigan, Bill's biographer: "I've never understood why he didn't want me to write it. I was so mad, and hurt. I don't think I have ever gotten over it. It still makes me mad just to think about it." (*BWB,* 114)

Bot. "We want to leave you with the feeling that no situation is too difficult and no unhappiness too great to be overcome." An important caveat is found on page 108, bottom paragraph.

Page 105

Top. "Our loyalty and the desire that our husbands hold up their heads and be like other men have begotten all sorts of predicaments." Unmanageability begets unmanageability. The terror, bewilderment, frustration and despair (151) that defines an alcoholic in his cups likewise engulfs the family itself. Much of this is outlined on the initial four pages of the chapter.

Page 106

Mid. "They struck the children, kicked out the door panels, smashed treasured crockery, and ripped the keys out of pianos." Too often abusive or aggressive behavior is seen through the lens of alcoholism (i.e., it will go away when he or she stops drinking), rather than as a problem of power or control requiring its own treatment plan.

Page 108

Mid. "We realize some men are thoroughly bad-intentioned, that no amount of patience will make any difference." For a portrait of family dysfunction, as well as a personal glimpse at Bill and Dr. Bob, see Sue Smith Windows' account of her marriage to Ernie Galbraith ("a devil-may-care young fellow"; 158, bottom), in *Children of the Healer - The Story of Dr. Bob's Kids.* Ernie's story, "The Seventh Month Slip," appeared in the first edition of the Big Book.

Bot. *"One:* Your husband may be only a heavy drinker." One who satisfies the diagnostic criteria of alcohol abuse – not dependence.

Page 111

Top. "The first principle of success is that you should never be angry." Don't believe I can embrace this principle. It's one thing to experience anger; quite another to remain captive to it or allow bitterness and resentment to rule the day.

Top. "Patience and good temper are most necessary." Act out of your power, don't react out of your powerlessness.

Mid. "Do not set your heart on reforming your [partner]. You may be unable to do so, no matter how hard you try." Guard against setting yourself (and the family) up for more disappointment. Remember step one: "We admitted we were powerless over [the alcoholic] . . ."

Page 115
Bot. "Avoid answering these inquiries as much as you can." Don't enable!

Page 116
Mid. "We wives found that, like everybody else, we were afflicted with pride, self-pity, vanity and all the things which go to make up the self-centered person; and we were not above selfishness or dishonesty." Again, the alcoholic has no monopoly on the problem of self. From the Preface to *Lois Remembers,"* the memoirs of Lois Wilson:

> "Bill's recovery came about in spite of me. Although it was what I had been working for all our married life, I had gone about it the wrong way. My love, as deep as it was, was also possessive; and my ego was so great I felt I could change him into what I thought he ought to be."

Page 117
Bot. "Often you must carry the burden of avoiding [family dissension] or keeping them under control." The chapter often places the onus for the alcoholic's recovery squarely on his spouse. This strikes me as both unfair and counterproductive. It's certainly an invitation for resentment. It's one thing to be sensitive to, and understanding of, the needs and realities of one in the infancy of recovery, and quite another to be asked to shoulder a greater share of the responsibility for his or her recovery. This imbalance, if you will, is also commented upon by Francis Hartigan in his biography, *Bill W.:*

> "Had Lois [Wilson] written this chapter, it is quite likely that the content would have been different. The chapter Bill wrote seems to assume the ideal spouse to be someone with no other interest but the welfare of her husband, whereas Lois always had other interests. The chapter also seems to hold the spouse substantially responsible for maintaining her alcoholic husband's emotional stability and a positive outlook once he stops drinking. The futility of such a life, and the depth of the anger produced by trying to live it, were among the lessons Lois had learned for herself as the result of her shoe-throwing 'epiphany.'" (114)

☞ The reader is referred to *Lois Remembers*, pages 98-100, for an account of Lois's own confrontation with her essential finiteness and the juggernaut of self-will.

Page 118

Bot. "We do not like the thought that the contents of a book or the work of another alcoholic has accomplished in a few weeks that for which we struggled for years. At such moments we forget that alcoholism is an illness over which we could not possibly have had any power." See also "The Family Afterward": "While grateful that he drinks no more, they may not like the idea that God has accomplished the miracle where they failed. They often forget father was beyond human aid." (128)

Page 120

Top. ". . .but just as things are going beautifully he dismays you by coming home drunk. . .Though it is infinitely better that he have no relapse at all. . .it is by no means a bad thing in some cases." Therapeutic relapse or one that may result in a more rigorous working of AA program and principles. (*NA*, Fourth edition, 70)

Mid. "Cheer him up and ask him how you can be still more helpful." Again, the chapter seems to place an undue share of responsibility for the alcoholic's abstinence on his or her spouse. For example, cautioning that: "The slightest sign of fear or intolerance may lessen your [partner's] chance of recovery. In a weak moment he may take your dislike of his high-stepping friends as one of those insanely trivial excuses to drink." (120) Walking on eggshells more likely makes for resentment than reconciliation.

Bot. "God has either removed your [spouse's] liquor problem or He has not. If not, it had better be found out right away. Then you and your [partner] can get right down to fundamentals." Better still, let your partner get down to fundamentals with his or her sponsor, AA group, counselor, treatment provider, etc. You go to Al-Anon – or take the kids on that family vacation you've likely postponed for way too long!

Chapter 9

The Family Afterward

Summary - Speaks of the many challenges and readjustments facing family members of the recovering alcoholic. Observes that AAs "absolutely insist on enjoying life"; encourages the use of "fine doctors, psychologists, and practitioners of various kinds"; and stresses the importance of living by spiritual principles as a means of restoring trust and integrity with family members.

Page 122
Top. "Our women folk have suggested certain attitudes a wife may take with the husband who is recovering." Much of what "our women folk have suggested" applies equally to "attitudes a [husband] may take with the [wife] who is recovering."

Top. "This involves a process of deflation." Letting go of trying to impose one's will or one's own agenda on other family members.

Mid. "And why? Is it not because each wants to play the lead? The alcoholic has no monopoly on "selfishness – self-centeredness," on being a "producer of confusion rather than harmony." (61) See again the discussion of the "Actor" on pages 60 to 62.

Bot. "A doctor said to us, 'Years of living with an alcoholic is almost sure to make any wife or child neurotic. The entire family is, to some extent, ill.'" Less "ill" perhaps than "simply heroically responding to the chronic illness of alcoholism as well as they can." (*FA, 7*)

Page 124
Mid. "We think each family which has been relieved owes something to those who have not. . ." Step twelve: carrying the message to the families who still suffer.

Mid. "Cling to the thought that in God's hands, the dark past is the greatest possession you have – the key to life and happiness for others." A similar sentiment is found in one of the Twelve Promises: "No matter how far down the scale we have gone, we will see how our experience can benefit others" (84), and the last paragraph of Foreword To Third Edition.

Page 126
Mid. "He is straining every nerve to make up for lost time." The old problem of self, here masquerading as industriousness or fiscal responsibility. There is no making up for spilled milk; there is only moving on and recovering in one's Higher Power's time. Trying to take shortcuts or schedule recovery around one's own timeframe and agenda, are blocks to step three and precipitating factors in many an alcoholic's relapse.

Bot. "It is of little use to argue and only makes the impasse worse." Argument is one thing, respectful confrontation another. The text may be unduly optimistic here, assuming that dad's (or moms) "periods of crankiness, depression, or apathy . . . will disappear when there is tolerance, love, and spiritual understanding." While appropriate expectations and spiritual principles make for a healthy and healing mix, frank and constructive talks also have their place. It is one thing to be respectful of a healing process; quite another to be held hostage to, or manipulated by, dad's recovery, i.e., "If we confront him, he might get angry and drink." Participation in Al-Anon, a family program or individual counseling may be of benefit in helping family members work step one and reclaim their power and own lives.

Page 129
Top. "If the family cooperates, dad will soon see that he is suffering from a distortion of values." An apparent by-product of spiritual growth. Thus from 130, top:

> "Those of us who have spent much time in the world of spiritual make-believe have eventually seen the childishness of it . . . We have come to believe [God] would like us to keep our heads in the clouds with Him, but that our feet ought to be firmly planted on earth. That is where our fellow travelers are, and that is where our work must be done."

Bot. "Even if he displays a certain amount of neglect and irresponsibility towards the family, it is well to let him go as far as he likes in helping other alcoholics. During those first days of convalescence . . . ." As already suggested, while realistic expectations and spiritual principles make for a sober mix, continued "neglect and irresponsibility" need not be tolerated.

Page 131
Top. "This means trouble, unless the family watches for these tendencies in each other and comes to a friendly agreement about them." A candid and constructive family discussion about roles and responsibilities is often indicated.

Page 132
Mid. "If newcomers could see no joy or fun in or existence, they wouldn't want it. We absolutely insist on enjoying life." Thus from Chapter 11, page 152:

> "Yes, there is a substitute [for liquor] and it is vastly more than that. It is a fellowship of Alcoholics Anonymous. There you will find release from care, boredom and worry. Your imagination will be fired. Life will mean something at last. The most satisfactory years of your existence lie ahead."

Bot. "But those of us who have tried to shoulder the entire burden and trouble of others find we are soon overcome by them." Remember step twelve: ". . .we *tried* to carry this message to alcoholics. . ." (Italics added.) It might be suggested that whether or when the message takes root is none of the alcoholic's business; it is up to God.

Page 133

Top. "It is clear that we made our own misery. God didn't do it." See again page 62, and the italicized lines on page 103, bottom.

Bot. "God has abundantly supplied this world with fine doctors, psychologists, and practitioners of various kinds. Do not hesitate to take your health problems to such persons." This would seem as good a spot as any to mention the apparent bias of some AAs against *treatment* for alcoholism. I'm not entirely sure what to make of these folks. Perhaps some suffer from a form of pride or arrogance that ought to be red flagged and tenth stepped: "*I* sobered up in AA!" Or perhaps some are simply jealous of the opportunities afforded others.

Regardless, it might be recalled that Bill advocated the building of special clinics for alcoholics as early as 1937, largely as general hospitals often refused admission to those diagnosed as alcoholic (*PIO*, 179-180). And then Bill himself had three treatments at Towns Hospital between 1934 and 1935. And Bill Dotson, "Alcoholics Anonymous Number Three," certainly had what looks like a rudimentary form of the "Minnesota Model" of treatment: admission to Akron City Hospital for detoxification (May 26, 1935), education on the allergy and obsession, contact with other alcoholics (Dr. Bob and Bill W.), introduction to a spiritual solution to his alcohol problem, and continuing care recommendation (Oxford Group participation). And Dr. Bob insisted on hospitalizing the new prospect at Akron City Hospital – this to help hold the man's attention and emphasize the idea of alcoholism as rooted in illness. (*DB*, 102)

My advice to the newcomer who runs into any such pride or prejudice at AA is found on page 84: "Love and tolerance of others is our code." (You might even want to check out another meeting.)

☞ I think it important to distinguish between an application of the twelve steps to a particular problem or concern and the use of the AA group itself for help with this problem or concern. For example, both the steps and AA group may be of great value in helping quiet an episode of stinking thinking or putting a long-standing resentment to sleep. On the other hand, while a twelve steps approach to healing from depression, sexual abuse, or an eating disorder may be of enormous benefit, I wouldn't recommend the AA group itself for therapy on any of these matters. This is not intended as a swipe at AA. To the contrary. One of AA's greatest triumphs and strengths is its steadfast singularity of purpose: "Each group has but one primary purpose – to carry its message to the alcoholic who still suffers." (Tradition Five, Second edition, 564). It is simply a reminder not to bring, if you will, your dental problems to the eye doctor. (See also the discussion of specific medications for the treatment of various mental illnesses in the study of Chapter 5, first paragraph.)

☞ The belief by some that AA is anti-psychology is noted in Appendix E., Myths & Misconception About Alcoholics Anonymous"

Bot. "One of the many doctors . . . told us that the use of sweets was often helpful. . ." Sweets may not only help satisfy a "vague craving" in the night; they may also become a substitute for that very craving itself. Recovering alcoholics must be mindful of cross-addiction: the tendency of their illness to seek partnership with an alternate source of "arousal, satiation, and fantasy." (*AP*, 3) From alcohol to food, food to cocaine, cocaine to gambling, spending or sex, this vulnerability will persist throughout their life. As noted by Nakken in *The Addictive Personality:*

> "Once an addictive personality is established within a person, the specific object or event of the addiction takes on less importance. When the Addict is firmly in control, addicted people can (and often do) switch objects of addiction as preferences change or as trouble arises with one particular object or event. Addicts who switch objects of addiction also know it's a good way to get people off their backs...The Addict side of their personality is very important for recovering addicts to understand because it will stay with them for life. On some level, the Addict will always be searching for an object or some type of event with which to form an addictive relationship. On some level, this personality will always want to give the person the illusion that there is an object or event that can nurture him or her." (25-26).

Page 134

Top. "Alcohol is so sexually stimulating to some men that they have overindulged." Alcohol is a central nervous system depressant that dulls the reflexes of ejaculation and erection. (*SS*, 112) Chronic use is associated more with impotency ("It provokes the desire, but it takes away the performance." *BFQ*, 214:11), then with infidelity, relaxation, and reduction of inhibition.

Mid. "Without saying so, they may cordially hate him for what he has done to them and to their mother." It is important that children and adolescents be given permission to talk *and feel* about their father's and mother's drinking. Participation in Alateen, a family program, counseling or therapy may be of great benefit to them.

Bot. "In time they will see that he is a new man . . ." Flexibility is important here. Trying to impose one's own timetable on family reconciliation is but another manifestation of the problem of self.

Page 135

Top. "Here is a case in point: One of our friends is a heavy smoker and coffee drinker." Reference to Earl T., whose story, "He Sold Himself Short," appears in the second to fourth editions. (www.silkworth.net)

Mid. ". . .so she nagged, and her intolerance finally threw him into a fit of anger. He got drunk." Thus from Earl's story:

> A few months after I made my original trip to Akron I was feeling pretty cocky, and I didn't think my wife was treating me with proper respect, now that I was an outstanding citizen. So I set out to get drunk deliberately, just to teach her what she was missing. ("He Sold Himself Short," Second edition, 293)

Mid. "Though he is now a most effective member of Alcoholics Anonymous, he still smokes and drinks coffee . . . She sees she was wrong to make a burning issue out of such a matter when his more serious ailments were being rapidly cured." Bill Wilson, Dr. Robert Smith, and Ebby Thacher each died from respiratory illnesses related to their nicotine dependence – *not* their alcoholism. Would that "she was wrong."

☞ From the Center for Disease Control:

- Cigarette smoking causes about one of every five deaths in the United States each year. Cigarette smoking is estimated to cause the following:
- More than 480,000 deaths annually (including deaths from second-hand smoke)
- 278,544 deaths annually among men (including deaths from second-hand smoke)
- 201,773 deaths annually among women (including deaths from second-hand smoke)

(www.cdc.gov/tobacco/data_statistics/fact_sheets/health_effects/tobacco_related_mortality/)

Chapter 10

To Employers

Summary - Effort to enlighten employers about cost and pervasiveness of alcohol problem in the workplace. Suggestions offered on intervention and referral. Cautionary word against enabling the alcoholic is also included.

Page 136
Top. "Among many employers nowadays, we think of one member. . ." Reference to Hank Parkhurst, an early champion of the Big Book project. Hank's story, "The Unbeliever," appeared in the first edition of the text. "To Employers" may have also been written by him. (*PIO,* 200)

Page 139
Bot. "To you, liquor is no real problem. You cannot see why it should be to anyone else, save the spineless and stupid." See again Chapter 2, page 20:

> "Now these are commonplace observations on drinkers which we hear all the time. Back of them is a world of ignorance and misunderstanding. We see that these expressions refer to people whose reactions are very different from ours."

Page 141
Bot. "State that you know about his drinking, and that it must stop." Instruction on intervention. Rudiments of employee assistance program appear on pages 141 to 14

Chapter 11

A Vision For You

Summary – Calls to attention the insidious sway of the merciless obsession, and the spiritually spent days of a life centered on the bottle. Identifies as "sufficient substitute" for liquor the fellowship of Alcoholics Anonymous. Provides an overview of Bill 's initial meeting with Dr. Bob, Dr. Bob's own release from the merciless obsession (last of the Four Founding Moments (*NG*, 33), and AA's earliest days in Akron. And ends with appropriate ruffles and flourishes, and a final serving of hope.

Page 151

Top. "The old pleasures were gone. They were but memories." Fixing on "what it was like" to the exclusion of "what happened" is referred to as euphoric recall, a memory distortion in which the call of "old pleasures" blinds one to the months or years of alcohol-sodden unmanageability. (*LG*, 122).

Mid. ". . . and a heartbreaking obsession that some new miracle of control would enable us to do it." This time will be different! "The idea that somehow, someday he will control and enjoy his drinking is the great obsession of every abnormal drinker." (30)

Mid. "The less people tolerated us, the more we withdrew from society, from life itself." It is not just her efforts to hide and sneak her drinking or the rebuke by others, not just a desire to avoid reference to the bottle or the need for hurried ingestion of her drug that turns the alcoholic from "society, from life itself." Alcoholism (and the addictive process in general) is a turning inward and away from the usual means of sustaining oneself emotionally and spiritually, of confronting one's troubles, and of quieting an unquiet soul. King Alcohol holds out the illusion of shortcut, of an easier, softer way (*AP*, 5, 15). He promises solution, he masquerades as a god. In embracing this illusion, the alcoholic turns her back to the world. She breaks *relationship* with self, family, community, and Higher Power. She retreats behind closed doors. A sign says: "Go away. I don't need you anymore."

☞ This withdrawing "from society, from life itself," is captured in these chilling words from the story, "The Independent Blond":

> "I had been drunk for nine days, sick and alone and desperate. They didn't need to tell me that alcoholism was a sickness. When you take a bottle and lock that door and go in by yourself, that is death." (Second edition, 535)

☞ In succumbing to the bottle's charm, the alcoholic also abandons herself: she abdicates to illusion the power and freedom and responsibility to be author of her own story; she denies herself the sweat and sweet victories of living life on life's terms; she cheats herself of possibilities and awakenings; she settles for crumbs.

Mid. "As we became subjects of King Alcohol, shivering denizens of his mad realm . . ." Step one powerlessness.

". . .the chilling vapor that is loneliness settled down. It thickened, ever becoming blacker." Step one unmanageability.

Page 152
Top. "Someday he will be unable to imagine life either with alcohol or without it . . . He will be at the jumping-off place. He will wish for the end." The bottle as mighty betrayer; the alcoholic as spiritually spent. The words themselves could well capture Bill's own anguish and despair just moments before his spiritual awakening in Towns Hospital.

Mid. "I know I must get along without liquor, but how can I? Have you a sufficient substitute?" The genius of AA is that it attends to the alcoholic – *not* her alcoholism. It understands the need to compensate her for laying down the bottle, the need to reward her abstinence with sobriety, and the need to substitute spiritual sustenance for denied spirits. (*AAC*) How is this accomplished? Connection. Thus from Foreword to Third Edition: "Each day, somewhere in the world, recovery begins when one alcoholic talks with another alcoholic, sharing experience, strength, and hope."

☞ Compensation is of course woven into the Twelve Promises (83-84). Its need is also highlighted in the following paragraph from "The Keys To The Kingdom":

> Keeping one foot in front of the other is essential for maintaining our arrestment. Others may idle in a retrogressive groove without too much danger, but retrogression can spell death for us. However, this isn't as rough as it sounds, as we do become grateful for the necessity that makes us toe the line, for we find that we are more than compensated for a consistent effort by the countless dividends we receive." (Second edition, 311)

☞ The idea of connection as the antidote to intoxication fits nicely into the notion of addiction as an intimacy disorder, with addiction as a turning to objects or events – *not* other people – for "solution" to life crippling or limiting problems; and recovery as a turning to connection with others as solution to both life crippling problems and bottle.

Mid. "There you will find release from care, boredom and worry. Your imagination will be fired. Life will mean something at last. The most satisfactory years of your existence lie ahead." And yet more promises! Again, the text is generously sprinkled with promises and messages of hope.

Page 153

Top. "The practical answer is that since these things have happened among us, they can happen with you." Installation of hope.

Mid. "Our hope is that when this chip of a book is launched on the world tide of alcoholism, defeated drinkers will seize upon it, to follow its suggestions." One such defeated drinker was Sylvia K., whose story, "The Keys of the Kingdom," initially appeared in the second edition:

> I stayed up all night reading that book. For me it was a wonderful experience. It explained so much I had not understood about myself and, best of all, it promised recovery if I would do a few simple things and be willing to have the desire to drink removed. Here was hope. Maybe I could find my way out of this agonizing existence. Perhaps I could find freedom and peace and be able once again to call my soul my own. (309)

Bot. "Years ago, in 1935. . ." May 1935.

". . .one of our number. . ." Bill Wilson.

". . .made a journey to a certain western city." Akron, Ohio

Bot. "From a business standpoint, his trip came off badly." A proxy fight to wrest control of the National Rubber Machinery Company "wound up in a law suit and bogged down completely." (154)

Page 154

Mid. "One dismal afternoon he paced a hotel lobby. . ." The Mayflower Hotel.

Bot. "With a shiver, he turned away and walked down the lobby to the church directory." For the first time since his spiritual awakening in Towns Hospital (December 1934), Bill Wilson is humbled by the specter of King Alcohol. He's bitter, discouraged and alone. (*PIO*, 135) He's afraid he will drink. Understanding that in carrying a message of recovery to other alcoholics he'd managed to stay sober himself, he sets out to find a kindred soul. (*AACA*, 65-66)

☞ It is important to understand that Bill Wilson's spiritual awakening or conversion experience did not transform him into a god. He was still a human being, a subject of and to life. He was not cured of alcoholism; he was not rid of his spiritual pests. Indeed, it might be argued that Bill's own ego and vainglory –fantasies of captaining vast empires which he would manage with the utmost assurance (1), and insinuating his way into a proxy fight to win control of the National Rubber Machinery Company (*PIO*, 133-34) – helped set into motion the very series of events that ended in him pacing the Mayflower Hotel lobby, gripped with the fear of relapse (*AACA*, 65-66) Again from Chapter 5 ". . . but we invariably find that at some time in the past we have made decisions based on self which later placed us in a position to be hurt . . .So our troubles, we think, are basically of our own making." (62)

Bot. "He would phone a clergyman." The Reverend Walter F. Tunks, Episcopal minister and a founding member of the Akron Oxford Group. (*BW*, 77) Why Bill picked Rev. Tunks is unclear. Perhaps, as Lois suggested, it was because Bill liked funny names. Or perhaps because the name reminded him of his favorite Vermont expression, "taking a tunk," which meant taking a walk. (*PIO*, 136) Or perhaps there was something of the divine hand in Bill's reportedly random selection. Regardless, Tunks proved to be the right person at the right time.

Page 155
Top. "His call to the clergyman led him presently to a certain resident of the town [Dr. Bob], who, though formerly able and respected, was then nearing the nadir of alcoholic despair." Not as quickly or directly as the text suggests, and AAs everywhere must be grateful to Bill for his perseverance. Bill explained his situation to Tunks and asked if the clergyman knew of an Oxford Grouper who might direct him to another alcoholic. (*AACA*, 66) Bill received a list of ten people; some were not home, others were of no help. (Ibid, 66) The tenth (Norman Shepard), however, suggested Bill contact Henrietta Seiberling, the daughter-in-law of former Goodyear Tire founder and president, Frank Seiberling. (*PIO*, 136-37) More important, at least from AA's vantage point, Henrietta was a personal friend of Bob and Anne Smith. For some time, she and fellow Oxford Groupers had been praying for Dr. Bob's separation from drink. When Bill phoned and introduced himself as a member of the Oxford Group and a "rum hound" from New York (*PIO*, 137), Henrietta thought their prayers had been answered and invited him right over. (Ibid, 137) Dr. Bob, however, was presently boiled as an owl and in no shape to meet this stranger from the East. So their initial encounter took place the following afternoon, Mother's Day (May 12), at Henrietta's residence, the gatehouse of the Seiberling estate. (Ibid, 138)

Mid. "A spiritual experience, he conceded, was absolutely necessary, but the price seemed high upon the basis suggested . . . He would do anything, he suggested, but that." Dr. Bob resists outing himself with friends and creditors. The problem of self, here masquerading as fear and false pride, continues to rule. Dr. Bob seeks "an easier, softer way." (58)

Bot. "Some time later, and just as he thought he was getting control of his liquor situation, he went on a roaring bender." Reference to Bob's relapse in route to the American Medical Association convention in Atlantic City in June 1935. Bob started drinking before the train left the station. (*PIO*,147)

Bot. "For him, this was the spree that ended all sprees. He saw that he would have to face his problems squarely that God might give him mastery [over his drinking]." Dr. Bob reaps the relapse of the "easier, softer way." Restitution and the leveling of pride cannot be avoided if he is to recover.

Page 156
Top. "One morning he took the bull by the horns and set out to tell those he feared what his trouble had been." With my apologies to Admiral David Farragut, "Damn the torpedoes, step nine ahead!"

Mid. "He has not had a drink since." June 10, 1935 (Founder's Day). Alcoholics Anonymous is born. Dr. Bob is 55 years old.

☞ Mitchell K., AA historian, cites newly found material that casts doubt on the validity of this date. Assuming the soundness of the material, Dr. Bob's last drink was more likely on or about June 17, 1935. See https://www.verywell.com/dr-bobs-last-drink-67388

Mid. "One day they called on the head nurse of a local hospital." Mrs. Hall at the Akron City Hospital. (*DB,* 81)

Bot. "'Yes, we've got a corker.'" Bill D., the "man on the bed". His story, "Anonymous Number Three" appears in the second to fourth editions of the Big Book.

☞ The painting, "The Man On The Bed," was created by Robert M., a volunteer illustrator for the *AA Grapevine.* Originally titled, "Came To Believe," it was renamed "The Man On The Bed" in 1973 (*RG,* 103). It is popularly regarded as depicting the first twelfth step call (if one excludes Bill's earlier work with other alcoholics, including Dr. Bob), with Bill D. being the "man on the bed," Bill W. the man who sat beside the bed, and Dr. Bob as the man standing by the dresser. (*Ibid,* 103) The painting currently hangs in Bill's old studio at Stepping Stones in Bedford Hill, New York.

Page 158
Top. "On the third day the lawyer gave his life to the care and direction of his Creator. . ." Step three.

☞ Bill D's hospital stay highlight a number of features common to most twelve-step-based treatment centers today: detoxification, education on the disease concept and twelve steps, interaction with other recovering alcoholics, and continuing care plan.

Mid. "That was June, 1935." Per his story, Bill D. entered Akron City Hospital on June 26, 1935 (Second edition, 184). His discharge date, July 4 (*PIO,* 154), marked the beginning of AA's Group Number One. (Editor's note, Second edition, 189) Bill D. remained abstinent until his death in 1954. (*PIO,* 154)

☞ Clarence S., the "Home Brewmeister," argued that the group he founded in Cleveland in May 1939 (*Ibid,* 203) was the first to assume the name, Alcoholics Anonymous (*Ibid,* 203) (Recall that the Fellowship as a whole took its name from its book, *Alcoholics Anonymous,* published in April 1939.)

Bot. "He proved to be a devil-may-care fellow whose parents could not make out whether he wanted to stop drinking or not." Ernie G., age 30. His story, "The Seventh Month Slip," appeared in the first edition of the Big Book. Sue Smith, Dr. Bob's daughter, married Ernie in 1941. For a narrative account of alcoholism as a family illness, and a glimpse of the "human" sides of Bob and Bill, see *Children of the Healer – The Story of Dr. Bob's Kids,* published through Parkside Publishing Company.

Page 159
Mid. "He now returned home." Bill returns to New York in September 1935. AA's Number Two Group is started.

Bot. ". . . it became customary to set apart one night a week for a meeting to be attended by anyone or everyone interested in a spiritual way of life." One of but three references to meetings found in the recovery portion of the text (the others on pages 15-16 and 162). Again, early thinking amongst AAs was that meetings, while "desirable," were not essential for recovery. (*DB,* 131, 136)

Page 160
Top. "Outsiders became interested. One man and his wife placed their home at the disposal of this strangely assorted crowd." T. Henry and Clarace Williams, Palisades Drive, Akron. (*NW,* 68) The Williams were friends of Dr. Bob and Henrietta Seiberling, and fellow Oxford Group members. (Akron AA's split with the Oxford Group came in the winter of 1939. (*DB,* 218) Till then its members had simply regarded themselves as the alcoholic squad of the Oxford Group.)

Page 161

Mid. "A community thirty miles away . . ." Cleveland. AA group was formed there in May 1939 by Clarence S.

Page 162

Top. "a well-known hospital. . ." Towns Hospital at 293 Central Park West, New York City.

Top. "Six years ago one of our number was a patient there." Bill Wilson.
Top. "We are greatly indebted to the doctor in attendance there." William D. Silkworth, MD

Mid. "Then, in this eastern city. . ." New York City.

Mid. "Some day we hope that every alcoholic who journeys will find a Fellowship of Alcoholics Anonymous at his destination." Estimated worldwide membership of 1,989,124 as of January 1, 1999. (*GSB*)

Page 163

Top. "We believe and hope it contains all you will need to begin." "The early expectation was that drunks would order the book, make surrender, and as they got back to their jobs and lives would help other drunks." (*VS* 12)

Top. "To duplicate, with such backing. . ." That is, the backing of a Power greater than oneself.

". . . what we have accomplished is only a matter of willingness, patience and labor." Yet another promise!

Top. "We know of an AA member who was living in a large community." Henry P.; Montclair, New Jersey. (*RG,* 134)

Mid. "He got in touch with a prominent psychiatrist." Dr. Howard of Montclair, New Jersey. *(Ibid,* 134) (This is the same Dr. Howard so instrumental in the text's pronoun shift – from *you* to *we* – discussed in Chapter 5, page 58.)

Bot. "Arrangements were also made with the chief psychiatrist of a large public hospital. . ." Dr. Russell E. Blaisdell, Rockland State Hospital in Rockland County, New York. (*Ibid,* 134)

Page 164

Mid. "This is the Great Fact for us." From Chapter 2, page 25:

The great fact is just this, and nothing less: That we have had deep and effective spiritual experiences that have revolutionized our whole attitude toward life, toward our fellows and toward God's universe. The central fact of our lives today is the absolute certainty that our Creator has entered into our hearts and lives in a way which is indeed miraculous. He has commenced to accomplish those things for us which we could never do by ourselves.

Bot. "Abandon yourself to God as you understand God." Step three.

Bot. "Admit your faults to Him and to your fellows." Step five.

Bot. "Clear away the wreckage of your past." Steps eight and nine.

Bot. "Give freely of what you find . . ." Step twelve.

Bot. " . . . as you trudge the Road of Happy Destiny." "Life is difficult," notes Scott Peck in the opening line of *The Road Less Traveled,* and life is something that continues to happen to people in recovery, regardless of the length of abstinence or the quality of individual sobriety. Hard times will be, and some days may seem worse than the best days drinking. A good AA program will not shelter the traveler from these realities. It is neither panacea nor a roadmap around the raindrops. Nor is the steps directed journey necessarily the easier, softer way. To the contrary. Turning one's will and one's life over to the care of a Higher Power, going against the self-centered grain, taking up what life leaves on one's doorstep each day – well, not exactly the stuff of avoidance and escape. The payoff then? In truth, each much discover this alone. Still, perhaps a partial glimpse is offered on the last page of Sylvia K's story, "The Keys Of The Kingdom":

The last fifteen years of my life have been rich and meaningful. I have had my share of problems, heartaches and disappointments, because that is life, but also I have known a great deal of joy, and a peace that is the handmaiden of an inner freedom. I have a wealth of friends and, with my A.A. friends, an unusual quality of fellowship. For, to these people, I am truly related. First, through mutual pain and despair, and later through mutual objectives and new-found faith and hope. And, as the years go by, working together, sharing our experience with one another, and also sharing a mutual trust, understanding and love – without strings, without obligation – we acquire relationships that are unique and priceless.

There is no more 'aloneness,' with that awful ache, so deep in the heart of every alcoholic that nothing, before, could ever reach it. That ache is gone and never need return again. Now there is a sense of belonging, of being wanted and needed and loved. In return for a bottle and a hangover, we have been given the Keys of the Kingdom. (Second edition, 312)

Appendix A.

TWELVE-STEP PRESCRIPTION FOR ALCOHOL OBSESSION

A Relationship With One Power   **FOR**   A Relationship With Another Power
Greater Than the Alcoholic   Greater Than the Alcoholic

Relationship With Group   Relationship With Bottle

CONNECTION IS ANTIDOTE TO INTOXICATION

Appendix B.

"Bottles Were Only a Symbol"

In Alcoholics Anonymous, the bottle comes to symbolize a life out of relationship with – blocked off from – one's Higher Power.

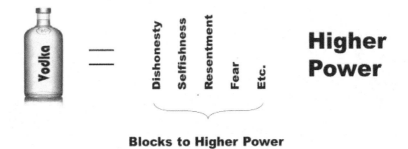

Appendix C.

Alcoholism as an Intimacy Disorder

If connection is antidote to intoxication – or fellowship "sufficient substitute" for the bottle (152) – then perhaps intoxication's allure is that of antidote to the emptiness, insufficiency, and loneliness of inadequate connection. From this standpoint, the bottle masquerades as both stand-in for rich relationships *and* comforter to whatever may ail. And from here, too, lies the idea of alcoholism (addiction) as an intimacy disorder: this turning and attaching to objects or events – *not* people – in hope of finding deliverance from one's story, one's problem, one's predicament. (Even in love addiction, the addict's partner is treated more as a prop than person in a mutually trusting and open relationship.) Why this avoidance of the "normal" ways of getting needs met? Why this attraction to things rather than connection with others? Let's take a look at the idea of attachment.

1.) Children have an inborn need to attach or form a strong emotional bond with their primary caregiver. This is an evolutionary adaptation designed to help ensure the child's safety, security and protection. Caregivers are also programmed to attach to their children, to nurture, teach and protect. Attachment theory holds that how children bond with their parents impacts their adult relationships, especially romantic relationships.

2.) Attachment is not just about the child's immediate need for safety and security. It is also essential for the child's emotional, social, and physical wellbeing and development

3.) There are four basic attachment styles between an infant and a *particular* caregiver: secure, avoidant, ambivalent, and disorganized. Roughly 65% of infants have a secure attachment style, 20% avoidant, 10-15% ambivalent, and 10-15% disorganized.

Attachment Styles	Rough Percentage (US)	Fulfillment of Child's Needs
Secure	65%	Believes and trusts needs will be met; feels safe, secure and protected.
Avoidant	20%	Subconsciously believes that needs probably won't be met.
Ambivalent (Anxious)	10 – 15%	Cannot rely on needs being met.
Disorganized	10 – 15%	Severely confused; no strategy to have needs met.

Reprinted with permission from http://www.positive-parenting-ally.com/attachment-styl

4.) Attachment patterns influences how the child – and then adult – regard themselves and their place in the world; how they problem solve and deal with life's challenges, changes and stresses; how they form and maintain friendships and romantic relationships; and how they regulate their emotional life. (www.positive-parently-ally.com/attachement-steyles.html) For instance, securely attached children tend to regard the world as a safe and stable place, one in which they are loved and in which their needs will be met. Children with insecure attachment styles may view the world as dangerous and unpredictable, as short on love and inconsistent in satisfying their needs.

5.) With secure attachments come rich relationships, emotional intimacy, positive self-regard, and a turning to others to celebrate the ups and cope with the downs. Insecure attachment styles, however, stymie the innate need to reach out when emotionally hungry or challenged, or when simply wanting to laugh and enjoy the company of others. Ambivalently attached individuals are generally reluctant to be intimate, worry whether their partner reciprocates their feelings, and become especially upset when a relationship breaks down; while avoidant individuals tend to withhold emotionally from social or romantic relationships. ("Attachment Theory – Styles and Characteristics; Cherry, Kendra; www.verywell.com; August 24, 2016).

Early environmental influences on a child's attachment style include: being a victim of abuse or neglect, or absent or intrusive parenting; assuming the role of adult in caring for a parent or sibling; acting as one' parent's confidant or surrogate partner (covert incest); being witness to the emotional, sexual or physical abuse or a sibling; and unresolved or unaddressed trauma. (From "Understanding Intimacy Avoidance" by Robert Weiss, MSW)

For "X" percent of individuals with an insecure attachment style, objects and events –
drugs and behaviors – masquerade as trusting substitute.

CONNECTION WITH KIND   **CONNECTION WITH THING**

SECURE ATTACHMENT   **INSECURE ATTACHEMENT**

6.) Of course, alcohol and drugs and other addictive pursuits are destined to boomerang, to turn back on one with often ferocious consequences. In lieu of relief or release from whatever may ail, the addict now finds himself the owner of two problems: the initial pain or predicament *plus* its "solution."

7.) For the alcoholic or addict with an intimacy struggle – one for whom the words connection and solution do not walk hand in hand – attending a twelve-step meeting or entering an outpatient or residential program may well seem a daunting prospect. To be vulnerable, to risk connection, may seem to open oneself to more harm; yet to stay the course seems almost unimaginable.

8.) The good news is that attachment styles are not fixed in stone. Alcoholics and addicts – people – can modify what attachment theorists refer to as *internal working models*. That is, beliefs, memories and expectations individuals hold about themselves, others, and their relationships with these others; messages and expectations that can contribute to their solitude, block their move into healthy connections, and keep alive their attachment to the bottle. ("Attachment Theory"; University of East Anglia; https://www.uea.ac.u/ providingasecurebase/ attachment-theory)

9.) Participation in AA has been correlated with increased secure attachment and reduction in avoidant and anxious attachment styles* -- not surprising when considering the program's emphasis on relationship building (fellowship and Higher Power), sponsorship, mutual support, home group attendance, humility and working with others. Too, the entirety of the twelve-steps menu speaks of relationship building or renewal: intra-personal, interpersonal, and Higher Power or spiritual. ("Alcoholics Anonymous Benefit and Social Attachment"; Smith, Bruce, and Tonigan, J.; Alcoholism Treatment Quarterly 27(2) 164-173, April 2009)

Connection Is Antidote To Intoxication

**"I know I must get along without liquor, but how can I?
Have you a sufficient substitute?"
Yes, there is a substitute and it is vastly more than
That. It is a fellowship in Alcoholics Anonymous." (152**

Appendix D.

Having Had a Spiritual Awakening

Perhaps, to borrow from Bill W. "there are as many definitions of spiritual awakening as there are people who have had them." (*12x12,* 106) This Appendix does not try to add to the bag of definitions, nor does it pretend to offer anything near a definitive word on subjects as vague and varied as spirituality, psychic change, spiritual experience and spiritual awakening. At best. it offers an "approximate" understanding of these ideas as found in the book, *Alcoholics Anonymous.*

Part I
Spiritual Awakenings:
What They Don't Do. What They Are Not.

Awakenings are generally not heralded by hip-hopping
angels, French horns, or the parting of rafters.
Nor are they generally in the nature of "sudden and
spectacular upheavals" or personality changes.
(*AA,* Appendix II)

Awakenings don't protect us from the hurts and blows
and messiness of life. They don't deliver us from
making mistakes, doing wrong, or needing to brush
our teeth. Nor do they provide a basket of bliss,
happy endings, or a roadmap around the raindrops.

Awakenings are not an escape from life's labors, or
the cure for whatever may ail (including addiction).
Nor do they signal or guarantee a lasting walk
on the sober side of the street.

In short, life continues to happen to
those who awake.

Part II
Spiritual Awakenings:
What They May Be

In 1926, a Roland Hazard travels to Switzerland to place himself under the care of Carl Jung, MD, for the treatment of his alcoholism (AA, 26-28). Believing Roland's situation "utterly hopeless," Jung nonetheless allows that a "vital spiritual experience" might offer his patient an exception to his devastating prognosis.

Roland subsequently finds this spiritual experience through his involvement in the Oxford Group, a non-denominational evangelical movement popular in Europe and North America at that time. (This was the same spiritual movement in which AA's co-founders, William "Bill" Wilson and Robert Smith, MD, would later discovery recovery."

What was (or is) this vital spiritual experience prescribed for Roland's alcoholism? In Chapter 2 of the basic text, Jung refers to these as "phenomena" in which "ideas, emotions, and attitudes which were once the guiding forces of" our lives "are suddenly cast aside, and a completely new set of conceptions and motives begin to dominate them." (27) Thus . . . "fear changes into faith, hate into love, egoism into humility, anxiety and worry into serenity, complacency into action, denial into acceptance, jealousy into trust, fantasizing into reality, selfishness into service, resentment into forgiveness, judgmentalism into tolerance, despair into hope, self-hate into self-respect, and loneliness into fellowship." (*PTP,* xi-xii)

> Another way to express or capture this spiritual change or shift in thinking, especially as pertains to recovery from an addiction, is as follows:

"I *can't* stay sober."	→	"I *can* stay sober."
"I can *not* drink."	→	"I *can* not drink."
"I feel hopeless."	→	"I feel hopeful."

This shift – a mix of spiritual, cognitive and emotional elements – has a profound impact on one's orientation to self and others. "I can't" stands with it back to the world, closed to contrary signs and signals, ever-renewing itself in its own despair. "I can" shouts "Yes" to the world, it's door open to people and possibilities, renewing itself through repeated challenges and adventures. "I can't" diminishes and depletes; "I can" expands and nourishes. I can't seeks out the comfort of the drug or bottle; I can sees its home in connections with others.

Additional examples of this shift in our life course or heading may be found in these excerpts from two Big Book stories:

> This latest part of my life has had a purpose, not in great things accomplished but in daily living. Courage to face each day has replaced the fears and uncertainties of earlier years. Acceptance of things as they are has replaced the old champing at the bit to conquer the world. I have stopped tilting at windmills, and instead have tried to accomplish the little daily tasks, unimportant in themselves, but tasks that are an integral part of living fully. ("He

Sold Himself Short," 285, Second edition)

I went to a meeting to see for myself this group of freaks or bums who [had written the Big Book and begun AA]. To go into a gathering of people was the sort of thing that all my life . . . had me feeling an uncomfortable outsider, needing the warming stimulus of drinks to join in. I went trembling into a house in Brooklyn filled with strangers . . . and I found I had come home at last to my own kind. There is another meaning for the Hebrew word that in the King James version of the Bible is translated "salvation." It is: "to come home." I had found my salvation. I wasn't alone anymore. ("Women Suffer Too," 228, Second edition)

Part III
Spiritual Experiences:
More About What They May Be

However defined (and again, this may best be left to angels dancing on the head of pins) several things should be noted about these awakenings, experiences, or psychic changes, as confusion on the subject may lead the reader or relative newcomer in recovery to develop unrealistic expectations about them – and hence either frustration or shame or both if they fail to materialize on his or her timetable.

• The majority of spiritual awakenings/experiences/psychic changes are "not in the nature of sudden and spectacular upheavals." (*AA,* Spiritual Appendix II). The majority of these experiences or phenomenon are what American philosopher and psychologist, William James, referred to as the "'educational variety' because they develop slowly over a period of time;" (Ibid.) and indeed "quite often friends of the newcomer are aware of the difference long before he is himself." (Ibid.)

• James did not believe "that direct divine operation is needed to bring such [spiritual experiences] about," and in fact argued that the value of any such spiritual conversion of change must be decided solely on empirical grounds, that is, the outcome vs. cause. (*VRE,* 189). Thus, Bill W's awakening or "white-light experience" during the course of his third treatment for alcoholism is no less significant if rooted in alcohol-induced psychosis (as skeptics have argued) than the divine. What shines is the positive attained for Bill – he never took another drink, he never again doubted the existence of God (*PIO,* 121) – and through him millions of others.

• Psychic or personality changes do not happen in a vacuum, but within the context of the individual's connections with others, community, and

Higher Power. Again, from Spiritual Appendix II:

> He finally realizes that he has undergone a profound alteration in his reaction to life; that such a change could hardly have been brought about by himself alone. What often takes place in a few months could seldom have been accomplished by years of self-discipline."

In other words, the spiritual or personality changes one begins to realize throughout recovery are not the ends of willpower or self-knowledge, but the fruits of connecting to the world. Were this otherwise, were the individual's finite power sufficient to bring about recovery, there would be little cause for peer-centered treatment, or mutual support groups such as AA and NA.

• Last, spiritual or conversion experiences are generally not the stuff of bouncy hayrides on sunny, summer days. Despite their varied manifestations, Bill W's reading of James' Varieties of Religious Experiences suggested three common characteristics (*PIO,* 124):

> **Calamity** – person has her own encounter with suffering or misfortune.

> **Admission of Defeat** – Each person has confronted the limits of her power.

> **Appeal to a Hight Power** – Each asks for help.

These three elements would later find expression in the "three pertinent ideas" on page 60 in the Big Book (*NW,* 24)

(a) That we were alcoholic and could not manage our own lives.
(b) That probably no human power could have relieved our alcoholism.
(c) That God could and would if He were sought.

They are also etched into these wonderful lines from page 50 of the text:

> "In the face of collapse and despair, in the face of the total failure of their human resources, they found that a new power, peace, happiness, and sense of direction flowed into them.

• While a spiritual awakening is undoubtedly "the result of these steps," the reader is advised to monitor their expectations: while *some thing* will undoubtedly occur after an initial go-around with them, blazing illuminations are the exception, not the rule. Too, spiritual experiences are not the sort of phenomena that appear on cue. It's one thing to claim "a profound alteration in his reaction to life" as the result these steps (*AA,* Appendix II); quite another to anticipate that this change will fall on a particular date and time. (It's not as if the newcomer works steps one to eleven, hits a tally button, and out pops a white-light experience.) Interestingly enough, awakenings may show at the start of one's journey, not just down the road.

IN THE BEGINNING

A woman attends her first AA meeting. Fear, loneliness and despair accompany her through the door. Shame almost blocks her way forward. She sits; she listens. Something surprising happens: she finds herself relating to the words, the stories, the consequences of a life centered around the bottle. Someone asks her if she'd like to share. She says no, then starts to cry. Support is offered; others tell of their first meeting, their cravings and fight with alcohol. She hears and is inexplicably, unexpectedly lifted from her solitude. Her thirst disappears. She fights against thinking; fights against accepting what is happening. "No," she cautions herself, "No. It can't be. Can't be possible. There can't be a way out for me, too. Can there?"

"Yes," she murmurs on her way home. "Yes," and again begins to cry.

Part IV
No Free Lunch

Spiritual awakenings do not bring an end to the work of recovery nor offer a pass to life's daily chores. They do not elevate us above the crowd, eliminate the need for wise teachers and good friends – or even regular checkups at the dentist. We still step in puddles, still bump our heads, still have our allotment of heartaches and troubles. Whatever awakenings may stir in us, whatever awareness or force or direction may startlingly or slowly appear, awakenings don't get us into heaven, keep us out of hell, or make us reservations to dine with the gods. (Remember, the next to final line of the Big Book refers to trudging the Road of Happy Destiny – *not* tripping the light fantastic.)

AWAKENING

A woman sits in treatment. It's now day 10. She's been here before. Is on course to be here again. She likes to drink. Finds no reason to stop. Her husband has his work, her children their schools and friends. Why should she be denied the bottle? Time goes by; some peers move on, new patients move in. One of these new patients tells his story; of putting his drinking ahead of his family, his addiction at the center of his life. How selfish of him, our friend unexpectedly finds herself thinking. How cruelly and utterly selfish.

And then it kicks: "That's me! I too have put all I've valued, and honored, and promised aside for a drink. I too have abandoned, and betrayed, and neglected for the sake of the bottle. My God, my family didn't sign up for this. They didn't consent to have a mom in name only; a drunk who masquerades as responsible citizen."

The next morning our friend shows for group. She's present. She's come to work.

"What's happened to you?" her therapist asks.

"Simple," our friend replies. "I woke up."

Appendix E.

Myths & Misconceptions About
Alcoholics Anonymous

- **AA Is the Only Way!** Who says? Certainly, *not* AA. It's important to separate what some members of AA may say from the words of the fellowship itself:

> "Upon therapy for the alcoholic himself we surely have no monopoly. Yet it is our great hope that all those who have as yet found no answer may begin to find one in the pages of this book and will presently join us on the highroad to a new freedom." (*Alcoholics Anonymous,* Foreword to Second Edition)

'N Other Words

Hey Pal,
Bar tab higher than your mortgage?
Can't remember where you parked your last two cars?
Dog runs for cover every time you return home?
First thing you reach for in the morning is the bottle –
not your partner, or kids, or even the toothbrush?
Just got let go from another job.

We *may* have an answer for you.

- **AA is anti-medication.** Who says? Not AA. Again, it's important to separate what some members of AA may say from the words of AA itself:

> "We recognize that alcoholics are not immune to other diseases. Some of us have had to cope with depressions that can be suicidal; schizophrenia that sometimes requires hospitalization; bipolar disorder, and other mental and biological illnesses . . .

> "It becomes clear that just as it is wrong to enable or support any alcoholic to become readdicted to any drug, it's equally wrong to deprive any alcoholic of medication which can alleviate or control other disabling physical and/or emotional problems." ("A.A. Member – Medications and Other Drugs"; 6)

- **AA is anti-psychiatry.** No again. From page 133 of the Big Book:

"God has abundantly supplied this world with fine doctors, psychologists, and practitioners of various kinds. Do not hesitate to bring your health problems to such persons . . . Try to remember that though God has wrought miracles among us, we should never belittle a good doctor or psychiatrist."

• **AA regards the alcoholic as blameless for his/her illness.** The idea of alcoholism as a *fault-free* illness is not found in the Big Book. Any number of illnesses exist for which individuals bear at least some responsibility for developing, and alcoholism – at least AA's understanding of it – may well be one of these. The Big Book argues that the alcoholic's inability to control his or her drinking is rooted in illness – *not* that the alcoholic plays no role in acquiring this illness. (See comment on mid-paragraph page 53 in *AA*.)

☞ There is no reference to alcoholism as a *disease* in "The Doctor's Opinion" or text portion of the Big Book (1 - 164). Alcohol use disorder is instead identified as an illness, malady or allergy. (The word disease appears but once, on the bottom of page 64: "From [resentment] stem all forms of spiritual disease . . .")

• **The 12-step philosophy is incompatible with a holistic approach to recovery.** AA (all 12-step programs) are advocating a spiritual solution to the alcohol problem; that is, a solution rooted in relationship with a Higher Power or fellowship of kindred souls. Nothing in this prescription is antagonistic toward therapies or treatments that help advance individual well-being, or defuse impediments to emotional intimacy or relationship building. It simply argues for a spiritual remedy to the alcoholic's craving for a drink.

• **AA keeps one sober.** Sorry, it's not the AA program or fellowship that provide a defense against the first drink. Rather, it's one's *relationship* or *connection* to program and fellowship that helps defuse the power of addiction's call. Just walking into a meeting won't get one sober any more than just walking into a bar will get one drunk. Want to get lit up? You have to do something: drink. Want to get sober? You have to do something here as well: connect. As is repeatedly noted throughout this guide: connection is the antidote to intoxication. (It's only drugs that hold out the illusion of *something for nothing.*)

☞ Remember: The third pertinent idea on page 60 reads, "That God could and would [relieve the alcohol obsession] *if he were sought.* (Italics added.)

Appendix F.

"Dr. Silkworth's Rx for Sobriety"

Anyone who tried to impress a drinking alcoholic with the approach, "You can't have your cake and eat it, too," would probably draw a scornful, "So what! Who wants any caked? Tony, make it a double this time."

The same idea expressed as, "you can't have your bottle and drink it, too," might get his attention because to a drinking alcoholic a fresh unopened bottle, brimming brightly with abundance, is a symbol of good things to come. He knows well enough, of course, that he can't drink it and still have it, but he blocks his mind to the inevitability of that horrible moment when the last bottle with be empty.

The untapped bottle remains a symbol to the non-drinking alcoholic, at least to the alcoholic who has dried up in A.A. So long as it stands unopened it represents drinks he has not taken – and the good things of life he has found by not drinking.

Yet, now and then a persevering soul tries to have both the figurative and the liquid contents of the bottle. He tried to make an impossible compromise.

In the opinion of a man who has administered personally to at least 10,000 alcoholics, the attempt to make this kind of compromise is one of the most common causes of failure to get a safe hold on A.A. Dr. W. D. Silkworth, genial and beloved little patriarch at Towns Hospital, New York, for 12 years and now also in charge of the new A.A. ward at knickerbockers, also New York, defines it as the "alcoholic double-cross."

"The majority who slip after periods of sobriety," says Dr. Silkworth, "having double-crossed themselves into thinking that somehow they can have the unopened bottle and drink it, too. Even though they have been in A.A. and going to meetings, and following parts of the program, they have accepted it with reservations somewhere. They actually have been one step ahead of a drink. Then they began playing around with the notion they can drink a little and still have the good things of A.A. The outcome is as inevitable as the bottle becoming empty once is has been opened by the alcoholics."

When Dr. Silkworth discussed A.A. "slips" his usually cheerful face becomes serious, even a little grim. Through his long years of practice in the field, he has become increasingly sympathetic, but not case-hardened, to the alcoholic. He understands what they experience. Having been one of the first in his profession to support A.A. and having guided scores of alcoholics into A.A. during the last 10 years, he also appreciates the fact that a "slip" for an A.A. involves an extra degree of remorse and misery.

Dr. Silkworth is particularly emphatic on one point.

"'Slips' are not the fault of A.A. I have heard patients complain when brought in for another 'drying out,' that A.A. failed them. The truth, of course, is that they failed A.A.

"But this mental maneuvering to transfer the blame is obviously another indication of fallacious thinking. It is another symptom of the disease."

A quick way to get Dr. Silkworth's appraisal of A.A. is to ask him how he thinks "slips" can be prevented.

"First," he explains, "let's remember the cause. The A.A. who 'slips' has not accepted the A.A. program in its entirety. He has a reservation, or reservations. He's tried to make a compromise. Frequently, of course, he will say he doesn't know why he reverted to a drink. He means that sincerely and, as a matter of fact, he may not be aware of any reason. But if his thoughts can be probed deeply enough a reason can usually be found in the form of a reservation.

"The preventive, therefore, is acceptance of the A.A. program and A.A. principles without any reservations. This brings us to what I call the moral issue and to what I have always believed from the first to be the essence of A.A.

"Why does this moral issue and belief in a power greater than oneself appear to be the essential principle of A.A.? First, an important comparison is found in the fact that all other plans involving psychoanalysis, will power, restraint and other ingenious ideas have failed in 95 per cent of cases. A second is that all movements of reform minus a moral issue have passed into oblivion.

"Whatever may be the opinions one professes in the matter of philosophy—whether one is a spiritualist or a scientific materialist—one should recognize the reciprocal influence which the moral and physical exert upon each other. Alcoholism is a mental and physical issue. Physically a man has developed an illness. He cannot use alcohol in moderation, at least not for a period of enduring length. If the alcoholic starts to drink, he sooner or later develops the phenomenon of craving. Mentally this same alcoholic develops an obsessive type of thinking which, in itself a neurosis, offers an unfavorable prognosis through former plans of treatment. Physically science does not know why a man cannot drink in moderation. But through moral psychology—a new interpretation of an old idea—A.A. has been able to solve his former mental obsession. It is the vital principle of A.A., without which A.A. would have failed even as other forms of treatment have failed.

"To be sure, A.A. offers a number of highly useful tools or props. Its group therapy is very effective. I have seen countless demonstrations of how well you '24-hour plan' operates. The principle of working with other alcoholics has a sound psychological basis. All of these features of the program are extremely important.

"But, in my opinion, the key principle which makes A.A. work where other plans have proved inadequate is the way of life it proposes based upon the belief of the individual in a Power greater than himself and faith that this Power is all-sufficient to destroy the obsession which possessed him and *was* destroying him mentally and physically.

"For many years I faced this alcoholic problem being sure of one scientific fact—that detoxification by medical treatment must precede any psychiatric approach. I have tried many of these orthodox psychiatric approaches and invented some new ones of my own. With some patients I would be coldly analytic, if they were of the so-called 'scientific' type who is apt to have a superior attitude toward anything emotional or spiritual. With others, I would try the 'scare' method, telling them that if they continued to drink they would kill themselves. With still others, I would attempt the emotional appeal, working both the patient and myself into a lather. He might be moved to the point of shaking hands dramatically and telling me, with tears streaming down his face, that he was never going to take another drink. And I knew that the probability was he would be drunk again within two weeks or less.

"Since I have been working with A.A. the comparative percentage of successful results has increased to an amazing extent.

"The percentage of success that A.A. has scored leaves no doubt that it has something more than we as doctors can offer. It is, I am convinced, your second step. Once the A.A. alcoholic has grasped that, he will have no more 'slips.'"

Sources

"A.A. At The Crossroads"; Delbanco, Andrew and Thomas; *The New Yorker;* March 20, 1995; page 62

AA The Way It Began; Pittman, Bill; Glen Abbey Book, Seattle, Washington; 1988

AA: The Story (A revised edition of *Not God: A History of Alcoholics Anonymous);* Kurtz, Ernest; Harper/Hazelden Book; San Francisco, California; 1988

Alcoholics Anonymous; Alcoholics Anonymous World Services, Inc., New York, New York; 3rd Edition (1976)

"Alcoholics Anonymous Benefit and Social Attachment"; Smith, Bruce M., Ph.D., and Tonigan, J. Scott; Alcoholism Treatment Quarterly, 27(2) 164-173, April 2009.

Alcoholics Anonymous Comes of Age; Alcoholics Anonymous World Services, Inc., New York, New York; 1957

The Addictive Personality; Nakken, Craig; Hazelden, Center City, Minnesota; Second Edition; 1996

"Attachment Theory"; Wikipedia; https://en.wikipedia.org/wiki/Attachment_theory

Awakening The Buddha Within; Das, Lama Surya; Broadway Book, New York, New York; 1997

Bartlett's Familiar Quotations; Kaplan, Justin, General Editor; Little, Brown and Company, New York, New York; 16th Edition; 1992

Big Book Discussion; McQuany, Joe and Parmley, Charlie; Gopher State Tape Library, St. Paul, Minnesota.

Bill W.; Thomsen, Robert; Hazelden, Center City, Minnesota; 1975

Bill W.: A Biography of Alcoholics Anonymous Cofounder Bill Wilson; Hartigan, Francis; St. Martin's Press, New York, New York; 2001

Box 1980; The AA Grapevine, Inc., New York, New York; 1999

"Bowlby's Attachment Theory"; McLeod, Saul; http://www.simplypsychology.org/bowlby.html; 2007

Courage to Change; Edited by Pittman, Bill, and B., Dick; Fleming H. Revell, Grand Rapids, Michigan; 1994

Centers for Disease Control and Prevention (CDC); www.cdc.gov

Children of the Healer; Smith, Bob and Windows, Sue Smith; Parkside Publishing Corporation, Park Ridge, Illinois; 1992

Compton's Encyclopedia Online v3.0; © 1998 The Learning Company, Inc. *Desk Reference to the Diagnostic Criteria from DSM-5;* American Psychiatric Association, Washington, DC; 2013

Dr. Bob and the Good Oldtimers; Alcoholics Anonymous World Services, Inc., New York, New York; 1980

Ebby; The Man Who Sponsored Bill W.; B., Mel; Hazelden Pittman Archives Press; Center City, Minnesota; 1998

The Encyclopedia of Philosophy; Edwards, Paul, Editor in Chief; Macmillan Publishing Co., Inc. & The Free Press, New York, New York; 1967

The Family and Alcoholism; Kellermann, Joseph L.; Hazelden, Center City, Minnesota; 1984

General Service Board of Alcoholics Anonymous, Inc.; New York, New York

Healthy Devil Online; © 1997-99 Duke University.

The Language Of The Heart; The AA Grapevine, Inc., New York, New York; 1988

Lois Remembers; Al-Anon Family Group Headquarters, Inc., New York, New York; 1987

Loosening The Grip; Kinney, Jean, and Leaton, Gwen; The C.V. Mosby Company, Saint Louis, Missouri; 1978.

New Wine; B., Mel; Hazelden, Center City, Minnesota; 1991

Not-God; Kurtz, Ernest; Hazelden, Center City, Minnesota; 1979

The Oxford Group & Alcoholics Anonymous; B., Dick; Glen Abby Books, Seattle, Washington; 1992

Parabola; Volume 12, Number 2, May 1987; pages 56-67

A Program For You; Hazelden, Center City, Minnesota; 1991

The Psychopathology of Denial; Hazelden, Center City, Minnesota; 1981

Pass It On; Alcoholics Anonymous World Services, Inc., New York, New York; 1984

"The Four Infant Attachment Styles"; www.positive-parently-ally.com/attachement-steyles.html)

Prepublication (Multilith) Copy of the Big Book; General Service Office of Alcoholics Anonymous, New York, New York; 1939

The Promises of Sobriety; C., Cecil; Hazelden, Center City, Minnesota; 1987

Practice These Principles and What Is The Oxford Group?; Hazelden Pittman Archives Press, Center City, Minnesota; 1997

A Reference Guide To The Big Book Of Alcoholics Anonymous; C., Stewart; Recovery Press Inc., Seattle, Washington; 1986.

The Road Less Traveled; Peck, M. Scott, MD; Touchstone, New York, New York; 1978

Research Update; Butler Center For Research And Learning; Hazelden Foundation, Center City, Minnesota

Sexual Solutions; Castleman, Michael; Simon and Schuster, New York, New York; 1980

Silkworth – The Little Doctor Who Loved Drunks; Mitchel, Dale; Hazelden, Center City, Minnesota; 2002

The Spirituality of Imperfection – Storytelling and the Search for Meaning; Kurtz, Ernest and Ketcham, Katherine; Bantam Books, New York, New York; 1994

Turning Point; B., Dick; Paradise Research Publications, San Rafael, California; 1997

Twelve Steps And Twelve Traditions; Alcoholics Anonymous World Services, Inc., New York, New York; 1952

"Understanding Intimacy Avoidance"; Weiss, Robert, MSW; http://www.robertweiss.com/about-sex-addiction/intimacy-avoidance/

Victims & Sinners – Spiritual Roots of Addiction and Recovery; Mercadante, Linda A.; Westminster John Knox Press, Louisville, Kentucky; 1996

Women Pioneers in Twelve Step Recovery; Hazelden Pittman Archives Press, Center City, Minnesota; 1999

"Russell Forrest's *Big Book Study Guide* is an enormous benefit to anyone who has a serious interest in the book, *Alcoholics Anonymous*. It is extremely well organized, it teaches and provides new insights from the first to the last page. I highly recommend it."

~ Craig Nakken, MSW
Author, *The Addictive Personality*

"I can think of no one better suited to write a commentary on the Big Book of Alcoholics Anonymous than Russell Forrest. He brings to the task two decades of experience working at Hazelden with a broad spectrum of patients afflicted with the illness of chemical dependency. A wise and accomplished practitioner, Forrest's commentary suggests valuable insights into the wisdom of the Big Book, and offers clear directions to those seeking to understand the Twelve Steps and the recovery journey mapped out by them."

~ Damian McElarth, Executive VP of Hazelden Services, Ret.
Author, *Hazelden – A Spiritual Odyssey*

Russell Forrest, MA, CSAT, CCAC was the supervisor of Hazelden's extended residential program from 1984 to 2000. In 2003 he journeyed to Canada to help launch the Sunshine Coast Health Centre in Powell River, British Columbia. In addition to *Big Book Study Guide,* he is a co-author of "Childhood Sexual Abuse - A Survivor's Guide for Men." He belief that "our stories tell us what we need to do" is a cornerstone of his clinical work. He enjoys sailing and riding the roads of the Colorado plateau. He currently lives in Halifax, Nova Scotia, miles and years from his birthplace in New York City.

Made in the USA
Las Vegas, NV
14 January 2023

65625697R00103